Microsoft Word Guide for Succ

From Basics to Brilliance in Achieving Faster and Smarter Results [II EDITION]

Copyright © 2023-2024

Kevin Pitch

TABLE OF CONTENTS

INTRODUCTION

Microsoft Word is a powerful tool. It's more than just a word processor. With the right knowledge, you can use it to create stunning documents, manage your work, and even impress your bosses and colleagues. That's what this guide is all about.

Microsoft Word comes with a database of formulas, functions, and charts that will help you streamline your tasks in less time. This software has everything from determining how much to charge for a product to calculating the optimal number of hours for a project. Now with the latest Word, you'll save time by doing the math for yourself, no more struggling to memorize formulas or painstakingly enter numbers by hand! You can prepare reports and research papers that will astonish your superiors and colleagues. Of course, your boss will depend on you for accurate statistics, but you'll have all the time in the world to put on a goldfish bowl.

Have you ever noticed that Word is missing some of the needed features? Have you noticed that Microsoft Word has consistently received complaints about its lack of features and seeming unwillingness to improve? Well, you are in the right place to get help. This book will teach you aspect of using Microsoft Word in ways it never intended and unlock more than 100 new customizations for your computer. In addition, it will teach you many advanced techniques like macros, keyboard shortcuts, and VBA scripts that make using the software easier than ever before.

The purpose of this book is simple. We want to give you practical solutions. We're not here to bore you with long definitions. Instead, we'll show you how to do things. By the end of this book, you'll know how to use the most helpful formulas, functions, and charts in Microsoft Word. You'll be able to optimize your tasks and surprise everyone with your Word skills.

Now, let's talk about the structure of this book. We've organized it in a way that makes sense, starting from the basics and moving to more advanced topics. First, we'll help you get started with the installation and setup of Microsoft Word. Then, we'll give you a comparative overview of Microsoft Word against other popular word processors.

We'll also dive into the features of Microsoft Word in Microsoft 365. This will give you a clear understanding of how Word works in the cloud and the benefits of using it. From there, we'll move to the nitty-gritty details of creating and managing documents, understanding the Word dashboard, and mastering page dimensions and margins.

But that's not all. We'll also share tips and tricks for formatting and editing, using styles, and working with numerations and bulletins. You'll learn more on the power of 'Find and Replace' function, how to effectively use the footer and header, and the best ways to insert images and tables.

Graphs and charts? We've got you covered. We'll show you how to create and customize them in Word. Plus, we'll discuss common problems and mistakes and how to avoid them. We'll guide you through creating a table of contents, image list, table list, and index. And, of course, we'll talk about error checks, print and export options, and the amazing track changes feature.

Collaboration is key in today's work environment. So, we'll delve into Word's collaborative tools, including sharing, co-authoring, and resolving conflicts. We'll also touch upon accessibility features, ensuring that your documents are accessible to everyone.

Security is paramount. We'll guide you through Word's security and privacy features, including password protection and permission management. And for those who love automation, we'll introduce you to macros and how they can make your life easier.

Integration with other Microsoft Office applications is a breeze, and we'll show you how. If you ever face issues, our troubleshooting and support section will come in handy. We've also included a section on strategic shortcuts and a frequently asked questions (FAQs) segment to address common queries.

This book is your one-stop-shop for everything related to Microsoft Word. We've packed it with valuable information, ensuring that every page you turn offers something new. So, let's dive in and start our adventure in the world of Microsoft Word.

1 GETTING STARTED: INSTALLATION AND SETUP

Starting with Microsoft Word can feel a bit overwhelming. But don't worry, we're here to make it easy for you. Think of Word as a tool, and like any tool, it's all about knowing how to use it.

So, you've decided to step up your game with Microsoft Word. Great choice! This software is a game-changer for many professionals. Whether you're drafting a report, creating a resume, or even writing a book, Word is the go-to tool for many. But before we dive into the advanced stuff, we need to ensure you have the basics down. That means starting with the installation and setup.

1.1 Installation Process

Installing Microsoft Word is a breeze. If you've ever installed an app or software on your computer, you're already ahead of the game. For those who are new to this, no worries, it's as easy as pie. First, you'll need to purchase Microsoft Word or get a subscription to Microsoft 365, which includes Word among other useful apps. Once you've made your purchase, you'll be given a download link. Click on it, and the installation process will begin. Follow the on-screen instructions, and in a few minutes, the software will be ready to use on your computer.

Installation Guide for Microsoft 365 on a PC

Step 1: Downloading Microsoft 365 or Office

1. Visit www.office.com.
2. Press on "Sign in" located towards top right.
3. Key in the email and password for your account linked to your Microsoft 365 purchase. This could be a Microsoft account, work, or school account.
4. Once signed in, based on your account type:
   - **For Microsoft Account Users:** a. Click "Install apps" on the Microsoft 365 home page. b. Click "Install" or "Install apps>" depending on your version.
   - **For Work or School Account Users:** a. Click "Install apps" on the home page. b. Choose "Microsoft 365 apps" to start the download.

Step 2: Choosing the Right Version

- By default, 64-bit version will download.
- If you have a 32-bit version of Microsoft 365, Office, Project, or Visio already installed, the 32-bit version will download instead.
- To switch between 32-bit and 64-bit:
   1. Uninstall your current version of Microsoft 365.
   2. Go back to www.office.com and sign in.
   3. Click on "Other install options."
   4. Pick your preferred language and version (64 or 32-bit).

Figure 1: Choosing your version

     5. Click "Install."

Step 3: Installing Office

1. Once the download is done, open the file. How you do this depends on your browser:
   - **Edge or Internet Explorer:** Click "Run."
   - **Chrome:** Press "Setup."
   - **Firefox:** Press "Save File."
2. If there is a pop-up window asking, "Do you want to allow this app to make changes to your device?", press "Yes."
3. Wait the installation to finish. You'll know it's complete when a pop up appears saying "You're all set! Office is installed now" and a short animation.

Step 4: Activating Microsoft 365 or Office

1. Click Start button located towards bottom left of the screen.
2. Type the name of the Microsoft 365 app you want to open, like "Word."
3. Click on the app's icon that appears.
4. When the app opens, agree to the license terms.
5. Your Microsoft 365 or Office is now active and ready!

Troubleshooting:

- If the installation takes too long or you face other issues, click "Need help?" on the installation page for a list of common problems and solutions.
- If you see the Activation Wizard when you open an app, follow its steps to finish activating your software.

Step-by-Step Guide to Installing Microsoft 365 on a Mac

Step 1: Downloading Microsoft 365 or Office

1. Navigate to www.office.com.
2. If not signed in yet, press "Sign in."
3. Enter the credentials of the account linked to your Microsoft 365 or Office purchase. This could be a school/work/Microsoft account.
4. Depending on the account type:
   - **For Microsoft Account Users:** On Microsoft 365 home page, press on the "Install Office."
   - **For School/Work Account Users:** On Microsoft 365 home page, press the "Install Office," then choose "Office 365 apps."

Step 2: Installing Microsoft 365 or Office

1. After downloading, open Finder and navigate to "Downloads."
2. Double-click the file named "Microsoft Office installer.pkg". (Note: There could be slight variations in the name.)

Tip: If an error occurs showing the file can't be opened having originated from unidentified developer, give it 10 seconds, shift it file to the desktop, hold down Control, and press the file to start installer.

3. In installation window, click "Continue."
4. Read software license agreement and press "Continue."
5. Press "Agree" as an indication that you are in acceptance of the terms.
6. Choose your preferred installation type and click "Continue."
7. To adjust disk space or shift the install location, review the details and press "Install." *Note:* To install particular Microsoft 365 apps only, click "Customize" and deselect the apps you don't desire.
8. If prompted, enter the Mac login details and press "Install Software."
9. Wait for the installation to finish, then click "Close."

Step 3: Activating Microsoft 365 or Office

1. In the Dock, press Launchpad icon to view all apps.
2. Select Microsoft Word icon (or any other Microsoft 365 or Office app).

3. A "What's New" window will appear when you open Word. Press "Get Started" to activate.

Additional Tips: Pinning App Icons to the Dock
1. Head to Finder > Applications. Open your desired Office app.
2. While in the Dock, either right-click or Control+click the app icon.
3. Select "Options" and then choose "Keep in Dock."

1.2 Initial Setup and Customization

Now that you've got Word installed, it's time to make it yours. Setting up Word to suit your preferences makes working on it a lot more enjoyable. Start by opening the software. On the top right, you'll see a 'File' tab. Click on it and then select 'Options'. This will open a new window with a list of customization options. Here, you can alter the default font, adjust the spell check settings, and even pick a theme for your Word interface. Spend a few minutes exploring these options and adjust them to your liking.

1. Understand the Default Language Behavior:
- Office will automatically install language version aligning to the Windows user locale as set on every computer.
- You are free to modify this default behavior to help in managing multiple language versions.

2. Customization Options:
- Install multiple languages on one computer.
- Choose specific languages for users' computers, irrespective of their operating system's language.
- Apply custom settings across all language versions within your organization.
- Implement various languages for different user groups.
- Add proofing tools for extra languages.

3. Initial Language Settings:
- When launching an Office app for first time, you will notice that default settings are applied based on the installed language and the Windows user locale.
- Adjust these settings utilizing Office Customization Tool (OCT), Group Policy, or the Language Settings tool.

4. Download Language Packs & Proofing Tools:
- For the latest Office versions, download an ISO image of language packs and proofing tools from the Volume Licensing Service Center (VLSC).
    1. Visit the Microsoft Volume Licensing Service Center and sign in with a business email.
    2. Click "Software Downloads" under Home tab.
    3. Choose the desired product, e.g., Office Professional Plus.
    4. Define your download method and desired language.
    5. For the "Operating System Type," pick 32/64 bit and click "Continue."
    6. A list of available downloads will appear. Choose the required package and download the ISO image.

1.3 Word Extensions & Templates

When you save a file on your computer, you might notice a few letters after the dot. That's called a file extension. Think of it like a label. It tells the computer what type of file it is. For Microsoft Word, there are different file extensions. Let's talk about them.

Microsoft Word has been around for a long time. Before 2007, when you saved a Word document, it had a ".doc" at the end. This ".doc" is a file extension. It's like a name tag for the file. It tells the computer, "Hey, I'm a Word document!"

But then, things changed in 2007. Microsoft Word got a new file extension. It's called ".docx". It's still a Word document, just a newer version. So, if you see a file with ".docx", you know it's a Word document from 2007 or later.

Now, there's another interesting file extension. It's called ".docm". The "m" stands for macro. Macros are like little programs in Word. They help you do tasks faster. If a Word document has a macro, it will have ".docm" at the end.

But what if you want to make a template in Word? A template is like a blueprint. It's a starting point for other documents. For templates, Word uses the ".dotx" file extension. So, if you see ".dotx", you know it's a Word template.

Templates, on the other hand, are pre-made document designs. Instead of starting from scratch, you can pick a template that fits your needs. Whether it's a business letter, a resume, or a birthday card, there's a template for it. To access templates, click on 'File' tab, select 'New', and one can see a list of templates available. Choose one, and you're good to go.

What's a Template? We define a template as a pre-designed document one can utilize to start a new document quickly. It sets the structure, including fonts, styles, and layout. Every Word document starts from a template, often the default one named "Normal.dotm". When one saves a given file as a template, it gets the ".dot" extension.

Why Use Templates? Templates save time. If you often create similar documents, templates ensure consistency and speed up the process. They can also set up specific editing environments for different tasks. The more detailed your template, the less you'll need to add later.

What's Inside a Template? Templates can have:
- **Styles**: These remain even if the template is lost.
- **AutoText**: Doesn't copy to new documents.
- **Macros and Custom Toolbars**: Available if the template is accessible.

Types of Templates in Word
1. **Normal.dotm**: Loads every time you open Word.
2. **User Templates**: You can load these when needed.
3. **Workgroup Templates**: Also manually loaded.
4. **Global Templates**: Auto-load with Word and are in the startup folder.
5. **Non-file based templates**: Internal to Word; users can't modify.

Where Are Templates Stored? You can set specific locations for templates. They don't need to be on a shared drive. Subfolders in template directories create new tabs in Word. Templates in top-level folders show on the General tab. Prefix a template with an underscore to prioritize it.

The Default "Blank Document" The standard blank document is based on the "Normal" template. If you don't pick a template, Word uses "Normal.dotm". Once a document is made from a template, later changes to the template won't affect that document. Word pulls text and styles from templates into documents but not macros.

Working with Templates Changes to a template don't impact existing documents. To always load a template, put it in the startup folder, making it a global template.

How to Open a Template To edit a template, open it from within Word. If you double-click a template file outside Word, it creates a new document from that template.

Template Options
- Set default folders for user and workgroup templates.
- Choose to get a prompt to save changes to the "Normal" template when closing Word.

In summary, file extensions are like name tags for files. They tell the computer what type of file it is. For Microsoft Word, there are different extensions like ".doc", ".docx", ".docm", and ".dotx". Each one has its own purpose. Knowing them can help you understand and use Word better.

Remember, next time you save a Word document, check the file extension. It will tell you a lot about the file. And if you're ever in doubt, just think back to this section. It's all about understanding the basics of Word extensions and templates.

2 COMPARATIVE OVERVIEW

When we talk about word processing tools, Microsoft Word often comes to mind. It's like the popular kid in school. But just like in school, there are other kids, each with their unique strengths. In the world of word processing, there are tools like Google Docs and Apache OpenOffice. Each of these tools has its own set of features and benefits. So, how do they stack up against Microsoft Word?

2.1 Microsoft Word vs. Google Docs

Microsoft Word has long been the go-to word processing tool for many in offices and homes for years. From Austin, Texas, to New York City, people use it to write letters, create reports, and draft documents. It's known for its robust features and user-friendly interface. But in Silicon Valley, California, another tool is making waves. It's Google Docs. Google Docs has risen as a strong competitor, especially for collaborative work. Google Docs is a cloud-based word processor. This means you can access your documents from any device, anywhere. No need to save it on a USB stick or email it to yourself. Plus, it's free! But it's not just about being free. Google Docs allows multiple people to work on a document at the same time. Imagine a team in Austin and another in New York working together in real-time. That's the power of Google Docs.

Microsoft Word and Google Docs have similarities, but there are many significant differences, too: Microsoft Word is best for writing a long, complex document or a series of related documents. (It has the most powerful tools for working with tables, charts, and images.)

Google Docs is the better choice if you're writing a long blog post or article. Though it doesn't have as many tools as Word, it has some key advantages for small- and mid-sized documents. For example, it's designed to help you write quickly and easily—with a clean, distraction-free interface that gets out of your way. And because Google Docs can be shared with others, it has powerful tools for making your work more collaborative.

Microsoft Word is the best choice for using styles and multiple columns (and for inserting notes and comments). Google Docs is great for quickly capturing ideas in a single long document. However, you won't have much use for styles or columns—unless you want to use them. (Although you can use Google Docs to create a long, single-column document, Word is a better choice for formatting, designing, and editing.)

Microsoft Word has support for many different types of documents, from newsletters to newspapers to instruction manuals. Google Docs is ideal for long—and potentially long-term—writing projects that require collaboration with multiple people. That said, it can display standard documents, too.

Microsoft Word is an excellent choice for people who already use Microsoft software. However, Google Docs is designed for anyone and everyone. (And it's available on any device, making it ideal for collaboration.)

Figure 2: Google Docs platform

Features and Capabilities
- **Word**: With over 30 years of development, Word boasts a vast array of technical features, from basic image placement to advanced tools like macros and mail merge. It offers superior text style options, image incorporation, footnotes, and table controls.
- **Google Docs**: While it covers most essential editing tools, Google Docs might seem limited to seasoned Word users.

User Interface
- **Word**: Its extensive feature set can make the interface overwhelming for beginners.
- **Google Docs**: Offers a more streamlined and user-friendly interface, ideal for those who need basic editing tools.

Platform and Accessibility
- **Google Docs**: Web-based and accessible on any desktop platform with a modern browser. Apps are available for Android and iOS. Requires internet unless set for offline access on Chromebooks.
- **Word**: Primarily a desktop application. It has an online version, but with limited features. Available for Windows and MacOS, with free clients for Android and iOS. Online access requires OneDrive backup or a Microsoft 365 subscription.

Cost
- **Google Docs**: Free for individual use. Business version (Google Workspace) starts at $6/user/month.
- **Word**: Stand-alone version costs $150 for one computer. Microsoft 365 Personal is $7/month or $70/year, usable on up to five devices. Storage space is more generous with Microsoft 365, while Google Docs offers 15GB free.

File Types
- **Word**: Files can be saved in multiple formats, including .doc and .docx.
- **Google Docs**: Files are saved in Google Docs format. To use in other word processors, they need to be exported to formats like .doc or .pdf.

Collaboration Features
- **Word**:
  - **Co-authoring**: Multiple users can edit simultaneously.
  - **Comments**: For feedback and discussions.
  - **Track Changes**: View edits by other users.
  - **Reviewing**: Built-in feature for suggesting and reviewing changes.
  - **Sharing**: Share via email or link with adjustable access levels.
- **Google Docs**:
  - **Real-time Collaboration**: Simultaneous access and editing with immediate visibility of changes.
  - **Commenting**: For feedback and discussions.
  - **Suggesting Mode**: Propose changes for the document owner to review.
  - **Permission Levels**: Control editing or viewing rights.
  - **Notifications**: Get email alerts for changes or comments.
  - **Chat**: Communicate in real-time within the document.

2.2 Microsoft Word vs. Apache OpenOffice

Microsoft Word and Apache OpenOffice Writer are two leading word processors. While Word is a staple in many professional settings, OpenOffice Writer offers a free alternative. Here's a brief comparison to help users decide which suits their needs best.

Apache OpenOffice is an open-source alternative to Word. Microsoft Word is a proprietary program owned by Microsoft.

Apache OpenOffice is available under the Apache 2.0 License. Microsoft Word is available only with a paid license directly from Microsoft or via a third party.

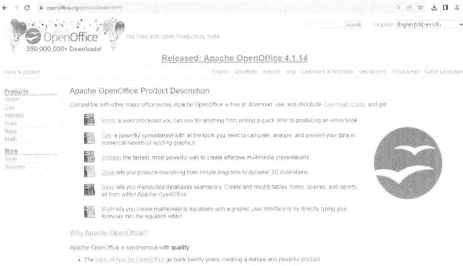

Figure 3: Apache OpenOffice

Features

Apache OpenOffice has almost all the same features as Word but has fewer templates and add-ins. Microsoft Word has more templates and other add-ins. Apache OpenOffice is designed with a different philosophy from Microsoft Word. Microsoft Word has a different philosophy than any other word processing program—emphasizing putting the tools you need in one place and a desire to help you write clearly and efficiently. Apache OpenOffice has a free, open-source Web-based version that you can use with your computer, smartphone, or tablet. Microsoft Word has a free Web-based word processor called Office Online. But it's designed for people who work on the Web and don't have a Mac or PC, and it lacks some of Word's advanced features like templates and Add-Ins.

- **Microsoft Word**: Known for its robust features, Word provides advanced text formatting, real-time collaboration, image editing, and a variety of export options. It's part of Microsoft Office suite, which integrates seamlessly with the other Microsoft applications.
- **OpenOffice Writer**: As a free, open-source word processor, Writer offers basic formatting tools, image insertion, and document export capabilities. However, it lacks real-time collaboration and some advanced features present in Word.

File Formats

Both Word and Writer support common file formats like Word documents, RTF, and PDFs. They also allow exporting to formats such as HTML and XML.

Collaboration

- **Microsoft Word**: Offers real-time collaboration, allowing users to share, track changes, and comment on documents.
- **OpenOffice Writer**: Doesn't support real-time collaboration.

Compatibility

- **Microsoft Word**: Compatible with Windows, Mac OS X, and mobile devices like smartphones and tablets.
- **OpenOffice Writer**: Works with Windows, Mac OS X, and Linux but doesn't support mobile devices.

Pricing

- **Microsoft Word**: Requires a paid subscription, with costs varying based on the version and package.
- **OpenOffice Writer**: Completely free to download and use.

Support
- **Microsoft Word**: Provides a comprehensive support system, including online forums, a knowledge base, and phone support.
- **OpenOffice Writer**: Offers online forums and a knowledge base but lacks phone support.

Apache OpenOffice has a smaller market share than Microsoft Word, but it's growing quickly. Microsoft Word has a larger market share than OpenOffice. But because it's expensive and proprietary, it has begun to lose market share to open-source programs like LibreOffice, OpenOffice, and Google Docs.

3 OVERVIEW OF MS WORD IN MICROSOFT 365 - A POWERFUL WRITING TOOL

Microsoft Word has several new features that make it a powerful writing tool. Among these features are OneNote and integration with other applications like Outlook. The latter offers a great deal of functionality when it comes to business writing. The new version also provides many features to help you organize your information. This will make the entire writing process easier.

Introduction Microsoft Office Suite

Microsoft Office Suite is a unique package that includes Excel, Word, PowerPoint, OneNote, and Outlook programs. It comes in different versions for different computing environments and includes mobile apps. In addition, there are web-based versions of some of the products. In 2011, Microsoft introduced Office 365, which competes with services such as Google Drive. Microsoft Office is a popular suite of applications used by most modern-day businesses. The applications are designed to simplify routine office tasks and improve work productivity. They are compatible with operating systems and are available in over 35 languages. Those looking for a business career may want to learn more about the suite. When comparing Office Suites, make sure to check the compatibility of each piece of software before making a purchase. Software within the same suite integrates better, eliminating the need to copy information. This is especially important for email clients, calendar apps, and scheduling systems. Having all your tools within the same family of products will reduce the likelihood of any communication issues. Microsoft PowerPoint is an excellent tool for creating exciting presentations. It offers many features, including the ability to insert images and text. You can also create attractive documents using Microsoft Excel. This program can also create tables and graphs. In addition to PowerPoint, Microsoft Excel offers various tools to assist you organize, store, and sort data. Microsoft Office also offers an online version. Microsoft 365 is a service that offers access to the office suite. Microsoft offers two software versions: Home & Student and Home & Business. Home & Student users only receive minor updates. Those who want more advanced features and functionalities should upgrade to the Home & Business version.

3.1 What is Microsoft Word in Microsoft 365?

Microsoft Word is a tool we all know. It's a word processor. But did you know it's part of a bigger family? That family is Microsoft 365.

The new release of Microsoft Word brings a slew of new features. The new feature called Smart Lookup helps you quickly look up a word's definition. It is a feature similar to Google's search bar but works inside Word. It allows you to search the web directly from the document and will even provide a preview of the word. Another great feature of this product is that it is free for Android and iOS devices. If you possess a Microsoft account, it is possible to use the mobile apps for both iOS and Android. However, if you want to use it on your desktop, you need to buy a subscription to Microsoft 365. You can download the program's free version online if you don't want to spend money on Word. It works in your web browser and syncs with cloud storage. However, it lacks some features that are available in paid versions. It's possible to edit a document from any computer, and sharing your files is easy. Word is a document app by Microsoft. It includes OneNote, which is designed for note-keeping. Word is more extensive and includes features like file attachments and sharing options. Word also supports the Grammarly add-in, which helps you improve your writing. A few of its other features are: OneNote supports drawing and audio recording. Microsoft Word can also open PDF files and save them in different formats.

Microsoft 365 is like a big box of tools. Inside this box, you find Word. But you also find other tools. There's Excel for numbers. There's PowerPoint for slides. And many more. All these tools work together. They're like a team.

Now, think of a toolbox. If you have a nail, you need a hammer. If you have a screw, you need a screwdriver. Microsoft 365 gives you the appropriate tool for the specific job. And Word is one of the most used tools in that box.

Word in Microsoft 365 is special. It's not just the Word we used years ago. It's better. It's smarter. It's connected. Let me explain.

When you write in Word, you can save your work. But where does it go? In the past, it went to your computer. Now, with Microsoft 365, it can go to the cloud. What's the cloud? Think of it as a magic place. It's where you can store things and get them from anywhere. So, if you write something at work, you can see it at home. It's that easy.

But there's more. Word in Microsoft 365 lets you work with friends. You can write together. At the same time! This is called collaboration. Imagine writing a story with a friend. You write one line. They write the next. You can see what they write as they write it. It's like magic.

Now, some of you might ask, "How much does this cost?" Good question. Microsoft 365 has a price. You pay every year. It's called a subscription. But for that price, you get many tools. Not just Word. And they all get updates. This means they get better over time.

Word in Microsoft 365 also has templates. What's a template? Think of it as a starting point. Let's say you want to make a birthday card. You could start from the scratch. Or you could utilize a template. The template gives you a design. You just add the words. It's a big time-saver.

Now, let's talk about looks. Word lets you change how your words look. You can pick different fonts. You can make words big or small. You can color them. And you can add pictures too. All this makes your work look great.

But what if you make a mistake? No problem. Word has spellcheck. It looks for mistakes and helps you fix them. It's like having a teacher inside the computer. And not just for spelling. It checks grammar too.

We talked about the cloud earlier. With the cloud, you can save your work. But you can also share it. Let's say you write a story. And you want your friend to read it. You can send them a link. They click it and read your story. No need to send big files.

3.2 How Microsoft Word works

Microsoft Word is like a magic pen. It helps you write, edit, and share your thoughts. But how does it work?

Microsoft Word is a word processing program allowing users to craft and edit documents easily. It also lets you keep track of changes and write notes in the margins of your documents. This feature helps create personalized documents like newsletters, meeting invitations, or general business correspondence. Microsoft Word also has features that allow you to create lists and spreadsheets. You can also download the Word app on your smartphone or tablet. You only need an internet connection and a Microsoft account to access it. The app runs inside your web browser and synchronizes with your cloud storage. However, there are some limitations to the free version of Word.

On opening Word, you will encounter a blank page. This is your canvas. Here, you can type anything you want. Stories, letters, or even a shopping list. As you type, the words appear on the screen. It's like magic, but it's just technology. Behind the scenes, Word is busy. It checks your spelling. It looks for mistakes. It even gives you ideas. All this happens in real-time. It's like having a helper with you.

Now, let's talk about the ribbon. It's the bar at the top. It has many buttons. Each button has a job. Some change the font. Others add pictures. And some make lists. The ribbon is your toolbox. It has everything you need. Word also lets you save your work. When you save, your words are safe. They won't get lost. You can come back to them anytime. And if you want, you can share them too. With friends, family, or the whole world. But what if you make a mistake? No worries. Word has an undo button. One click, and your mistake is gone. It's like it never happened. And if you change your mind, there's a redo button too. Pictures are fun. And Word lets you add them. You can pick any picture you want. From your computer or the internet. Once you add it, you can move it. You can make it big or small. You can even change how it looks.

Tables are useful. They help you organize things. In Word, making a table is easy. You pick how many rows and columns you want. Then you fill them in. You can add colors, borders, and more.

Now, let's talk about styles. Styles are like outfits for your words. They change how your words look. You can pick a style for headings. Another for quotes. And another for regular text. With styles, your document looks neat and tidy. Links are handy. They take you to other places. In Word, you can add links. To websites, files, or other parts of your document. When someone clicks the link, they go to that place. Word also cares about how your document looks. It lets you pick page sizes. You can add margins. And you can decide where the page breaks. All this makes your document look just right.

Now, what if you want to print? Word has you covered. It shows you a preview. So you know how it will look. You can pick how many copies you want. And which pages to print. Once you're ready, you hit print. And out comes your document.

Sharing is caring. And Word knows that. It lets you share your document. With anyone you want. They can read it. They can edit it. Or they can just leave comments. It's all up to you.

But what about safety? Word thinks about that too. You can include a password. Only people you trust can open it. You can also add watermarks. So, everyone knows it's yours.

Word is also smart. It can translate for you. Into many languages. It can also read aloud. So, you can hear your words. And if you're stuck, there's a help button. It answers all your questions.

In the end, Word is more than just a tool. It's a friend. It helps you express yourself. It makes your work look great. And it's always there for you. So next time you use Word, remember all the magic behind it. And enjoy every moment.

3.3 Subscription Plans and Purchasing

Microsoft 365 is a big deal. It's not just Word. It's many tools in one. Where do you get it? And what does it cost?

If you're wondering where you can buy Microsoft Word, we are here to help you. While this popular office suite used to be a one-time purchase, Microsoft has moved to a subscription model that makes more sense if you use multiple computers. The subscription model also includes freebies.

The price for this suite starts at $150 for a single installation. Subscription services to Office 365 start at $69.99 a year and include OneDrive and SharePoint. This package is ideal for students, teachers, and staff working in a school setting. Special offers are also available for students and staff at colleges and universities. When talking about word processing, most individuals and businesses think of Microsoft Word. It's easy to download, requires a Microsoft account, and allows you to edit your documents anywhere. Another great feature of this software is that it syncs with your cloud storage. It can also be used on cell phones, although it has some limitations.

1. Open your web browser, e.g., Firefox, or Google Chrome.
2. Head to the office website: www.office.com.
3. Click on **Get office** if you want an office or MS Word on your desktop and buy from the available options.
4. Install Microsoft Office, and MS word is available on your desktop for use.

First, Microsoft 365 is a subscription. That means you pay a fee. You can pay every month or every year. When you pay, you get access. You can use all the tools. And you get updates too. So, you always have the latest stuff.

There are different plans. Each plan has a price. The plans are for different people. Some are for students. Some are for families. And some are for businesses. You pick the one you need.

The Student plan is cool. It's for students. They get the tools for school. Word, Excel, and PowerPoint. They also get OneNote and Teams. It's great for homework and projects.

The **Family plan** is bigger. It's for up to six people. Everyone gets their own space. They can save their files. And they can share with others. It's good for families with many devices.

Business plans are different. They are for companies. Big and small. They have more tools. Like Exchange and SharePoint. These tools help companies work better.

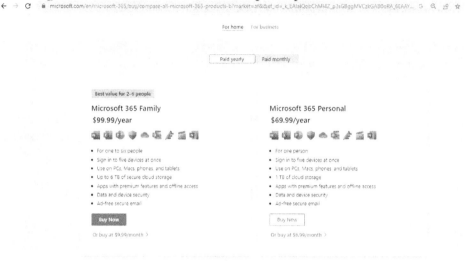

Figure 4: Microsoft 365 personal plans

Now, the price. Each plan has its cost. Student plans are cheaper. Personal plan goes for $69.99 per year or $6.99 per month. Family plans cost a bit more $99.99 per year or $9.99 per month. And business plans have different prices. The options include $6.00 per user per month, $12.50 per user per month, $8.25 per user per month and $19.80 per user per month. It depends on the tools you need.

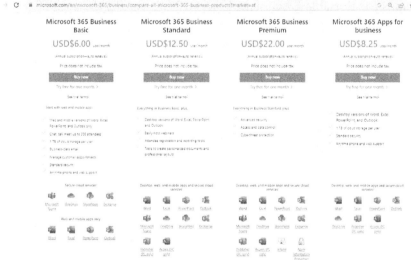

Figure 5: Microsoft 365 Business Plans

But wait, there's more. With Microsoft 365, you get cloud storage. It's called OneDrive. You can save your files there. And you can get them from anywhere. From your computer, phone, or tablet.

You also get security. Microsoft cares about safety. They protect your files. And they protect your data. So, you don't have to worry.

Buying Microsoft 365 is easy. You can buy it online. Go to the Microsoft website. Pick the plan you want. And pay with a card. You can also buy it in stores. Like Best Buy or Staples.

Once you buy, you get a key. It's a code. You use it to activate. Go to the Microsoft website. Enter the code. And you're good to go.

If you change your mind, that's okay. Microsoft has a return policy. You can get your money back. But there are rules. So, read them carefully.

Remember, Microsoft 365 is not just software. It's a service. You get support. If you have a problem, they help. You can call or chat. They are always there.

Updates are important. With Microsoft 365, you get them. They come automatically. You don't have to do anything. Your tools get better over time.

Some people ask, why subscribe? Why not buy once? Well, technology changes. New things come. And old things go. With a subscription, you stay updated. You always have the latest.

Also, with Microsoft 365, you can share. You can work with others. At the same time. It's called collaboration. It's great for teams. Everyone can see the changes. And everyone can add their part.

For those on a budget, there's good news. Microsoft offers discounts. For students and teachers. And for non-profits. So, check if you qualify.

In the end, Microsoft 365 is value. You get a lot for your money. Tools, storage, and support. All in one package. It's a smart choice for many. Whether you're a student, a family, or a business. Microsoft 365 has something for you. So, think about what you need. Look at the plans. And make your choice. It's an investment in your success.

4 CREATING AND MANAGING DOCUMENTS

4.1 Saving in Different Formats

Microsoft Word is a tool. It's a tool that helps us write. But sometimes, we need to share. And not everyone uses Word. So, we need options. We need to save in different ways. Let's talk about that.

When you write in Word, you create a document. That document has a type. It's called a format. The usual format is ".docx". But there are many others. And each has a purpose.

Why do we need other formats? Well, think about it. You might want to send a file. Maybe to a friend. Or to your boss. They might not have Word. So, you need a different format.

One popular format is PDF. It stands for Portable Document Format. It's great for sharing. Why? Because it looks the same everywhere. On a computer, phone, or tablet. It's like a photo of your document.

Then there's ".txt". It's a simple format. It has no pictures or fancy stuff. Just text. It's small and easy to open. Many programs can read it.

Another format is ".rtf". It stands for Rich Text Format. It's like ".txt". But it can have colors and styles. It's a middle ground. Not too simple, not too fancy.

Now, how do you save in these formats? It's easy. In Word, go to "File". Then choose "Save As". You'll see a list. The list has all the formats. Pick the one you want. Then click "Save".

But be careful. When you save in a new format, you might lose some things. Like animations or effects. So, always check your file. Make sure it looks right.

Also, remember your audience. Who will read your file? What tools do they have? If not sure, ask them. It's better to be safe.

For example, if you're sending a resume. Most companies like PDF. It's professional and clean. And they can't change it by mistake.

But if you're sharing notes, ".txt" might be better. It's simple and quick. And everyone can open it.

If you're working with a team, ".docx" is good. Everyone can edit and comment. It's great for collaboration.

There's also ".html". It's for websites. If you're making a web page, use this. It will look good in browsers.

And there's ".odt". It's for OpenOffice. It's a free program. Like Word, but different. Some people use it. So, it's good to know.

In the end, formats are tools. They help us share and work. They make our lives easier. So, learn about them. And use them well.

Remember, it's not just about writing. It's about communicating. And to communicate, we need to share. Formats help us do that. They help us reach more people. In more places. And in more ways.

So, next time you write, think about it. How will you share? What format will you use? And why? It's a small choice. But it can make a big difference.

Word offers a variety of file formats to save documents. Here's a summary:

- **Word Document (.docx)**: The standard format for recent versions of Word on both Mac and Windows.
- **Word 97-2004 Document (.doc)**: Compatible with older versions of Word on both Mac and Windows.
- **Word Template (.dotx and .dot)**: These are templates to start new documents. They save content and settings, with the ".dotx" being XML-based and ".dot" for older versions.
- **Rich Text Format (.rtf)**: A format readable by many applications, including other Microsoft programs.
- **Plain Text (.txt)**: This saves text without any formatting.
- **Web Page (.htm)**: For displaying documents on the web.
- **PDF**: A universal format that looks consistent across devices.
- **Word Macro-Enabled (.docm and .dotm)**: These are XML-based formats that preserve VBA macro codes, but the macros don't run across all versions.
- **Word XML Documents (.xml)**: will export contents to XML file, with versions compatible with Word 2007 and 2003 for the Windows OS.
- **Single File Web Page (.mht)**: A web display format that includes all elements in one file.
- **Word Document Stationery (.doc)**: Opens as a new, untitled document when accessed.
- **Speller Dictionaries (.dic)**: Used for custom dictionaries and exclude dictionaries.
- **Word 4.0-6.0/95 Compatible (.rtf)**: An RTF format for older Word versions.
- **Office Theme (.thmx)**: Saves the design elements of a file as a theme.

To use a theme from one document in another, go to Home tab, under Themes, and select the desired option.

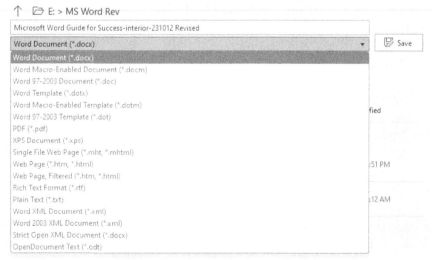

Figure 6: Different formats of saving

4.2 Recovering Lost Documents

Retrieve Deleted Word Documents on Mac:
1. Open Finder on your Mac.
2. Search the entire computer.
3. Double-click desired file. This opens it in Microsoft Word.
4. Go to File > Save As.
5. Rename the document and choose where to save it.
6. Click Save.

Restore Unsaved Word Documents while in Windows OS:
1. Open Microsoft Word.
2. Click on File > Info > Manage Document.

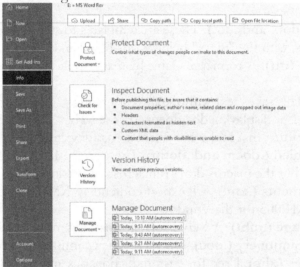

Figure 7: Manage Documents autorecovery

3. Choose "Recover Unsaved Documents."
4. You will see a list with unsaved Word documents appearing.
5. Select desired file and press Open.

Recover Lost Word Documents from Windows OneDrive:
1. Sign in to OneDrive.
2. Click on Recycle bin from the appearing menu.
3. Choose the Word document you wish to restore.
4. Click Restore.

Retrieve Unsaved Word Document:
1. Word can auto-save documents.
2. If a system crashes, unsaved documents might be lost.
3. Recover the unsaved files using Document Recovery, Temporary Files, Recycle Bin, AutoRecover, or Data Recovery.
4. Word backs up your work in the AppData folder.
5. Backup files have ".wbk" extension.
6. To check backup settings: File > Options > Advanced > Save > Always create backup copy.

Recover Deleted Word Documents via Backup:
1. Connect backup device to your computer.
2. Go to the Control Panel > System and Security > Backup and Restore.
3. Click "Restore my files".
4. Follow the Restore wizard.

Recover Deleted Word Documents in Previous Windows Version:
1. Search "File History" in Start menu.

2. Select "File History Settings".
3. Choose "Restore personal files".
4. Find the backup and click "Restore".

Recover Deleted Word Documents via Command Prompt:
1. Search "cmd" in Start menu.
2. Run as administrator.
3. Type chkdsk *: /f and press Enter. (* is your drive letter)
4. Type ATTRIB -H -R -S /S /D D:*.* command and press Enter. (Replace D with your specific drive)
5. Check for restored files.

Recover Deleted Word Documents via System Restore:
1. Search "create a restore point" in Start menu.
2. Select "System Restore".
3. Select a restore point and press "Next".
4. Confirm and click "Finish".
5. Note: System Restore might affect recent changes.

4.3 Document Versions and History

Microsoft Word is a tool many of us use daily. But did you know it has a feature that can save us from many headaches? That feature is called "Document Versions and History." Let's dive into it.

When Samantha was working on a big project for her company, she made several changes to her Word document. But then, she realized she liked her earlier version better. She wished she could go back in time. Well, with Microsoft Word, she kind of can!

What is Document History?
Document History is like a time machine. It lets you see older versions of your document. So, if you made a change yesterday but want to go back, you can!

Why is it Useful?
Imagine you're writing a report. You change a lot of things. But then, you think the first version was better. Instead of redoing everything, you can just go back. It saves time and stress.

How Does it Work?
Every time you save your document, Word remembers it. It creates a "snapshot" of that moment. These snapshots are your document's history.

Accessing Document History
To see your document's history, open your file. Then, click on "File" at the top. You'll see an option called "History" or "Versions." Click on it. You'll see a list of all the times you saved your document.

Going Back in Time
In the history list, you'll see dates and times. These are all the versions of your document. Click on any date to see that version. If you like it, you can restore it. It's that simple.

Safety First
This feature is like a safety net. If you make a mistake, you can always go back. It's like having multiple copies of your document. But you don't need to save them all. Word does it for you.

Keeping Track
Document History also helps you keep track. If you're working on a big project, you can see your progress. You can see how your document changed over time. It's like watching a plant grow.

Sharing and Collaborating
If you're working with a team, this feature is a lifesaver. Everyone can make changes. But if something goes wrong, you can always go back. It makes teamwork smooth and easy.

A Tip for Users
Always save your document regularly. The more you save, the more versions you have. It's like taking more photos on a trip. You'll have more memories to look back on.

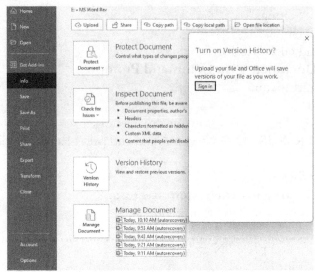

Figure 8: Version history

5   OPENING A BLANK DOCUMENT

Creating A New Document

MS Word will present you with a blank document to work on when you launch the application without opening an existing file. Simply type a word to place it on a page. You will eventually want to begin another fresh document, though. You have three options in Word for doing this:

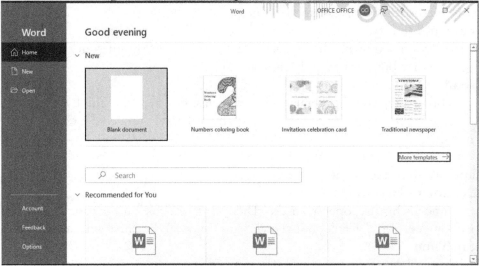

Figure 9: Opening the MS Word

1. The latest Word may seem a little overdone when you first start it up. This is because the Ribbon will take considerably more space than previous menus & toolbars. This modification might not be significant if you possess a huge screen. However, hiding the ribbon is possible by double-clicking the currently active tab if you intend to use a portion of this space. Then, click the tab whenever you need to view the ribbon elements.

2. Make a new, empty document. A basic, ornamental page is acceptable for creating a straightforward document, such as an essay of 3 pages, babysitting notes, or a news article. Alternatively, if you're just brainstorming and unsure of how your document will look in the end, you might choose to start with a blank table or structure the text using one of the Word templates.

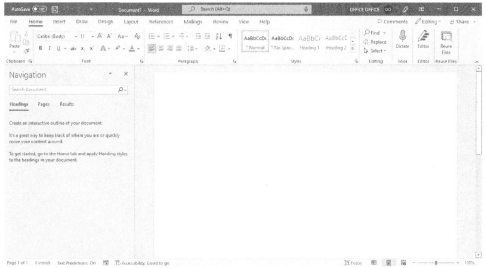

Figure 10: A new word document

3. It is possible to create a new one once you have opened an existing file. Utilizing a current paper as a starting point can help you save time. For example, you can reuse a letter format you like by altering its content repeatedly.

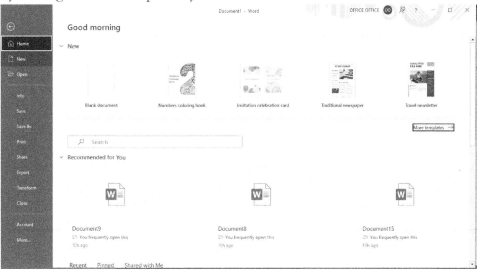

Figure 11: A new word document from File

5.1 Creating A New Blank Document

MS Word will always inform you whenever you launch the application, let's say you desire a brand-new blank document. ***No issue; here are the steps:***

1. Select File → New.

Figure 12: File button for new document

2. Click "Blank Document" in upper left-hand corner.
3. Do not become overwhelmed by the options in your New Document Box. You want to choose "Blank Document," which is in first row to the screen's left.
4. Click Create from the dialog box.

When dialog box vanishes, you see a blank page of a brand-new Word document.

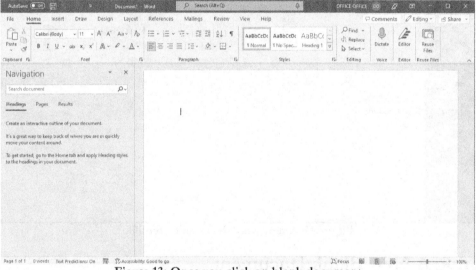

Figure 13: Once you click on blank document

Word provides options once your new document is open (File →New or using the shortcut Alt + F, N). For example, select Blank Document when you wish to open a blank document identical to one that is displayed when first launching the software. The previously produced document can also be opened with a new name through choosing "New from existing" instead.

5.2 Creating Your New Document Using A Template

Consider that this is the first time you are recording meeting minutes. You need well-formatted minutes but do not have access to any existing documents to assist you. Word is available to you, complete with templates.

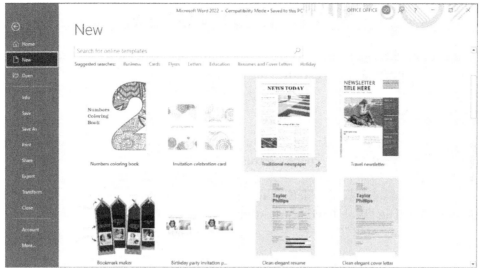

Figure 14: Creating new document from template

You access the previous month's minutes to conduct meetings using existing papers. Enter this month's minutes instead of the previous month's information. Similar principles apply whenever you utilize a template, but a template serves as a general document you may apply to various circumstances. Open and enter your text.

HOW TO OPEN AN EXISTING DOCUMENT

Here are the steps:

1. Select the File → Open button (Alt + F, O). Then, go to folder and choose file you wish to open.

Figure 15: Opening an existing document

2. The My Documents folder, where Word suggests you save your files, first appears in the Open window. Next, click the My Computer icon when your document is at a more remote place, and then go to the relevant folder.

3. Click Open after selecting the file.

Your document will open in Word after the Open box has vanished. You are prepared to begin working. Remember that you are overwriting the previous file whenever you save the opened document (you can use the shortcuts Ctrl + S, or Alt + F, S). Essentially, you are making a better, one-and-only copy of the document you just opened. You achieve this through Save As command (the shortcut is Alt + F, A) and rename if you wouldn't wish to overwrite your existing document.

6 VIEW OPTIONS

Microsoft Word is more than just typing. It's about seeing your work in the best way. That's why "View Options" is so important. Let's explore this feature.

6.1 Visualizing Options

When you open Word, you see your document. But did you know you can change how it looks? Yes, without changing the content! It's like changing the frame of a picture. The picture stays the same, but it looks different.

There's a tab called "View" at the top. Click on it. You'll see many options. "Print Layout" shows how it appears when printed. The "Web Layout" shows how it looks on a website. "Reading View" makes it easy to read without distractions. "Outline" lets you see the main points. Play around and see which one you like!

Microsoft Word has some good layouts you can use to view your documents in different situations. These layouts **are Web Layout, Read Mode, Print Layout, Outline,** and **Draft.**

- To choose a view mode, press **View** tab.

- Within the **Document Views** group, choose the view mode you desire.

Figure 16: View options

Below is the description of each of the view document groups:

- **Read Mode**: Provides a wonderful way of reading a document.

- **Print Layout**: This allows you to check the document appearance once you print.

- **Web layout**: Displays the appearance of a document as a webpage. Also, it helps whenever there are wide tables within the document.

- **Outline**: Displays the outline form where content appears as bulleted points. Comes in handy when creating headings and moving an entire paragraph in your document.

- **Draft**: This Layout switches your view to preview text without pictures (if any). It is helpful for quick editing since you only see the text.

6.2 Light Mode and Dark Mode

Ever worked late at night? The bright screen can hurt your eyes. That's where "Dark Mode" comes in. It changes the background to black. The text becomes white. It's easier on the eyes in low light. But during the day, "Light Mode" is better. It has a white background with black text. It's clear and easy to read. Switching is easy. Go to "File", then "Options". Click on "General". You'll see "Office Theme". Choose "Dark Gray" for Dark Mode. Choose "Colorful" for Light Mode. Simple!

Dark Mode
Do you know you can turn on dark mode on Microsoft Word, especially at night, to give your eye a break? The default background interface is the white mode. The Dark mode is designed explicitly for sight adjustment, mainly for night users and other purposes.

- To turn on dark mode, go to the top left corner and click on the **File** Menu.

- Within the file menu, move to bottom left corner and select Account. This opens up the account screen, and right in the middle is a section called **Office Theme.** By default, it's always on the colorful screen, which tends to be bright.

- Click on the drop-down arrow to see other colors (dark grey, white, black). You can select dark grey or black to make your screen dark

Note: When you change the office theme, not only will it affect word, it affects all other Office apps (excel and PowerPoint).

- When you go back to the word, all the ribbons tabs are dark, but the document still looks bright. To change this; Go to the **Design tab** locate to the right-hand side, and click on the page color. Next, click on theme color, and choose the dark color. Your document color changes to black, and word changes your font color automatically to white.

"Dark Gray" makes your Word background interface a little bit dark. You can select "Black" to get the "Dark mode" if you wish. Note that any change in your themes will also affect other Microsoft Suites such as Excel, PowerPoint, Outlook, and others.

Note: It doesn't affect your document when you want to print. It comes out in its standard color (white).

Figure 17: Dark Mode Theme selection

Changing the white document interface

Every of your theme settings or your customized theme settings can only affect the outlook, not the document content itself. To also change your white-board known as your document content area, simply follow these steps below:

- Go to your "Design tab."

- Under "Design," on your right-hand side, locate "Page Color" and click on it

Figure 18: Page color in design tab

- Then, you can select "Theme Colors" to "Black."

- Once you select "Color Black," your document content area will be on Black

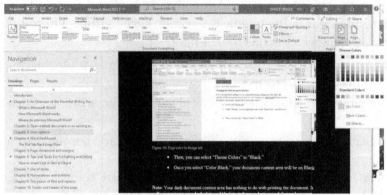

Figure 19: Black document interface

Note: Your dark document content area has nothing to do with printing the document. It will print out your standard white and black text, theme selection, and design document content. It only affects your Word interface, not with the copies to be printed.

Figure 20: Print option for Black document interface

Changing Views

Make use of these techniques to adjust the views:

- Click **one** of the 4 view options appearing on your status bar right side.
- Navigate to view tab>press **one** of the 5 options in your view group option, identify the immersive group, and click on the focus button.

The Read Mode

Changing to the Read mode helps you concentrate on the actual text and gives you a better view for proofreading. There is no option of entering or editing the text in Read mode. As the name implies, you can only read the text. All the icons are stripped away in this mode, the Ribbon, scroll bars, status bar, etc. All that will be displayed are the text and images (if any) contained in the document. It's a god consideration to use this feature when reading on a tablet.

Figure 21: Read mode activated

To exit read mode,

- Click **View** on menu bar at the navigation bar on your screen's top.
- Choose **Edit Document** from the list displayed.

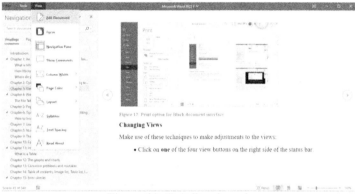

Figure 22: Exit Read mode

Print Layout view

Change the mode to Print Layout view when you anticipate to see or observe the entire document. With this option, you will see clearly how your document may appear on printing. Page borders, headers, footers, and even graphics can be seen clearly. You will also see where there might be a break in the page (marking the end of one page and the start of the next). In the Print Layout View, there is an option to click on **one page or multiple pages** on view tab to show extended details or less (as the case may be) on the screen.

The Web Layout view

Change to this view when you wish to have a feel of how the document should look like in the form of a web page. The background colors will be displayed (if one has been chosen before). The text will be coined to the window other than around the artwork within your document.

The Outline view

Change to this view when you plan to observe the organization of your work. With this option, we can only see or check headings within a given document. Allows easy movement backward or forward within the sections of your text. This simply means you can have the document rearranged in the Outline view.

The Draft view

Change to Draft view whenever you are writing a given document or wish to have more focus on the words. Shapes, pictures, and other images will be restricted as opposed to the read mode. You will not be able to see page breaks also. This view is best used when creating drafts.

Focus Mode view

Change to this view if you want reading to be easier and more fun. This view helps with preventing eye strain. All you can do in this view is enter text. All editing commands are taken off the screen. Press the escape key if you want to leave the Focus Mode view.

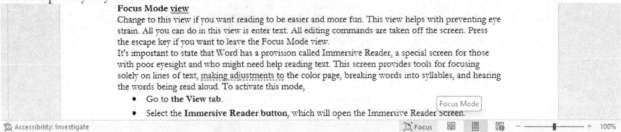

Figure 23: Focus mode view selection

It's important to state that Word has a provision called Immersive Reader, a special screen for those with poor eyesight and who might need help reading text. This screen provides tools for focusing solely on lines of text, making adjustments to the color page, breaking words into syllables, and hearing the words being read aloud. To activate this mode,

- Go to **the View tab**.
- Select the **Immersive Reader button**, which will open the Immersive Reader Screen.

6.3 Other Viewing Functionalities

Zooming is fun. Sometimes, you want to see a word up close. Other times, you want to see the whole page. The "Zoom" button lets you do that. It's like a magnifying glass for your document.

Gridlines are like the lines in a notebook. They help you place things neatly. To see them, click on "View". Then, check "Gridlines". Now, your document has a grid!

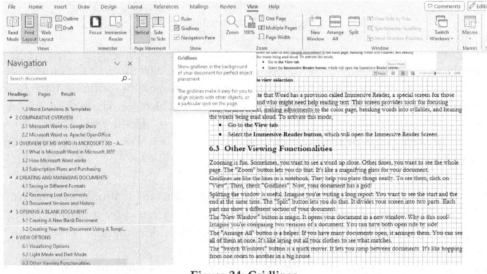

Figure 24: Gridlines

Splitting the window is useful. Imagine you're writing a long report. You want to see the start and the end at the same time. The "Split" button lets you do that. It divides your screen into two parts. Each part can show a different section of your document.

The "New Window" button is magic. It opens your document in a new window. Why is this cool? Imagine you're comparing two versions of a given document. You can have both open side by side!

The "Arrange All" button is a helper. If you have many documents open, it arranges them. You can see all of them at once. It's like laying out all your clothes to see what matches.

The "Switch Windows" button is a quick mover. It lets you jump between documents. It's like hopping from one room to another in a big house.

7 WORD DASHBOARD

Microsoft Word is a new word processor version allowing users to create and edit documents. In addition, this version includes a new Create PDF feature that will allow you to create and save a presentation in a PDF format. This format will allow you to share your presentation online or send it to others for review. You can also choose the action you want your document to take, such as print or send it as a PDF.

Save

A file has been saved from a computer's memory to a disk. It is usually used to refer to documents, spreadsheets, and other types of electronic files. Save often refers to the action of making an electronic copy of a document on disk so it can be retrieved later. Microsoft Word is among the famous word processors. It has many features and functions for writing professional documents, such as table of contents, generating indexes, and making on-the-fly grammar corrections. You can also create simple logos and letters. You can also insert graphics or sound in a document, such as a video or audio.

Save AS

This command, located in File menu of most applications, creates a copy of your document or image. However, unlike the regular Save command, which stores data back in the original folder or file, "Save As" creates a copy in a different location, format, and with a different or new name. Save-as command has several different uses. The first is for templates, which store text, styles, and keyboard shortcuts. The second is for a new document. When saved in this way, the template will be automatically created from a new document whenever one double-clicks on the file in Windows.

Another option is exporting a document to a PDF file. Such allows one to share the file with other users without sharing the original. Word has a WYSIWYG (What You See Is What You Print) display, which allows you to keep your screen's content consistent. This feature lets you copy and paste your content into other platforms without worrying about losing formatting.

Zoom In

The Zoom In a feature in Microsoft Word allows you to adjust the magnification of a document. When the magnification is set above the horizontal view limit, a horizontal scroll bar will appear at the bottom of the screen so that you can scroll and examine the document. You can get the Zoom In button on Ribbon's "View" tab. You can also toggle zoom levels using the + and - commands on the Zoom Control slider. When you click the Zoom button, a dialog box will appear, allowing you to adjust the zoom level. The default level is 100%. Other settings include 200% and 75%. When you change the zoom level, the percentage displayed on the Zoom slider will change.

COMPONENTS OF THE MS WORD

1. File

File-related options include New (for creating new documents), Open (for opening existing documents), Save, Save As, Print, Share, export, Info, and so on.

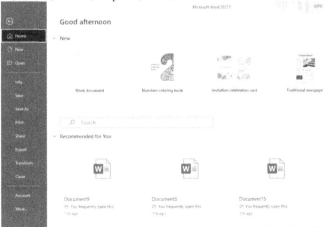

Figure 25: File tab options

2. Home

The default Microsoft Word tab is typically organized into 5 groups: the Clipboard section, Font group, Paragraph elements, Styles section, and Edit package. It provides an opportunity to customize the text's position, color, emphasis, font, and bullets. In addition, there are options such as font size, font color, font style, alignment, dots, space, etc. Apart from this, all the basic information needed to edit one's document is available in the Home options. It also has functions like the cut, copy, & paste. Once you select Home tab, the following alternatives will on display:

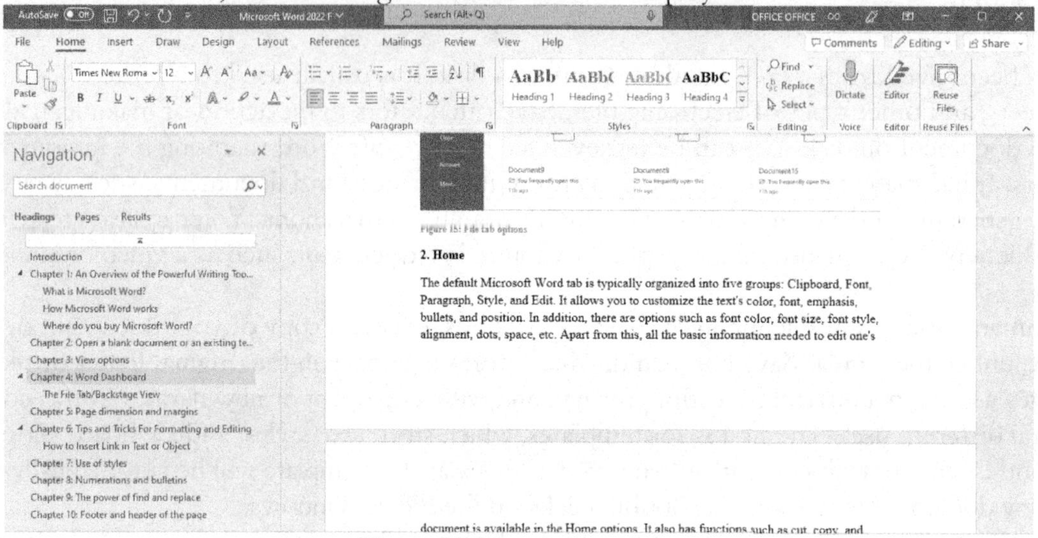

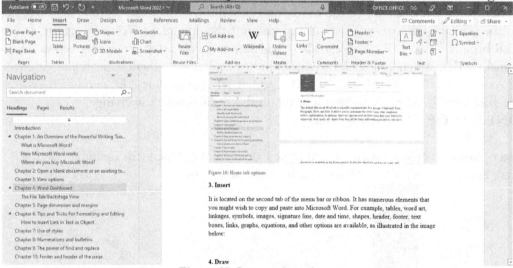

Figure 26: Home tab options

3. Insert

It is the second tab on ribbon with numerous elements that you might wish to copy and paste into MS Word. For example, tables, symbols, links, word art, equations, linkages, footer, signature line, images, header, shapes, text boxes, graphs, and other options are available, as illustrated in the image below:

Figure 27: Insert tab options

4. Draw

Stands as third tab on the ribbon. It is used in MS Word for freehand drawing. Provide the following kind of pens for drawing:

Figure 28: Draw tab options

5. Design

This is the fourth tab of the ribbon. The layout tab provides document layouts that you may choose from, such as left justification of text, page color, watermarks, and so on:

Figure 29: Design tab options

6. Layout

This serves as the fifth tab of the ribbon. It includes all of the choices for organizing the pages of your Microsoft Word document the way you desire. Establish margins, set indentation for paragraphs and lines, display line numbers, apply themes, line breaks, and so on, as seen in the image below:

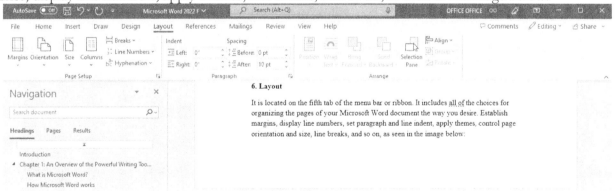

Figure 30: Layout tab options

7. References

It is the sixth tab in the ribbon or menu bar. The References tab allows you to insert references into a document and then generate a bibliography at the end. Typically, references are saved in a master list, which is used to add references to other documents. In addition, table of contents, footnotes, citations and bibliography, subtitles, table of contents, smart look, and other settings are available. You will get the following options after selecting the References tab:

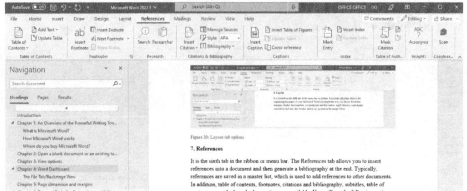

Figure 31: References tab options

8. Mailings

It is the seventh tab in the ribbon or menu bar. It is a less frequently used menu bar tab. This page allows you to design labels, print them on envelopes, merge mail, and so on. Following your selection of mail delivery, you will be presented with the following options:

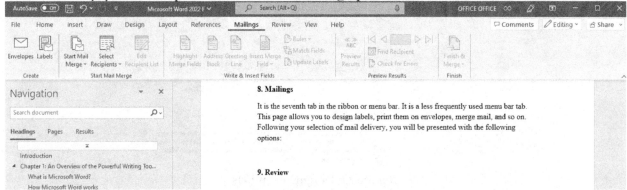

Figure 32: Mailings tab options

9. Review

It is the eighth tab in the ribbon or menu bar. The Review tab includes comments, language, translation, spell check, and word count options. It's handy for rapidly finding and editing comments. Following the selection of a review tab, you will be presented with the following alternatives:

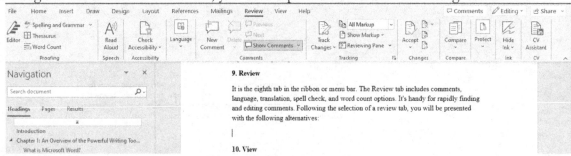

Figure 33: Review tab options

10. View

It is the ninth tab in the ribbon or menu bar. The View tab allows you to choose between facing and double pages and manipulate the layout tools. Print layout, outline, web layout, task pane, toolbars, ruler, header and footer, footnote, full-screen view, zoom, and other features are included, as shown in the image below:

10. View

It is the ninth tab in the ribbon or menu bar. The View tab allows you to choose between facing and double pages and manipulate the layout tools. Print layout, outline, web layout, task pane, toolbars, ruler, header and footer, footnote, full-screen view, zoom, and other features are included, as shown in the image below:

Figure 34: View tab options

QUICK ACCESS TOOLBAR

No matter which tab is selected, you may access common instructions using the Quick Access Toolbar, located directly above the Ribbon. You can add other actions as necessary, but it shows the Save, Undo, and Redo commands by default.

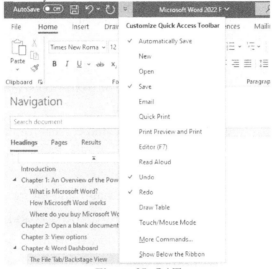

Figure 35: QAT

- Click the drop-down arrow to the right of the Quick Access Toolbar to add a command to the toolbar.
- Choose the desired command from the menu.

The Quick Access Toolbar will now include the command.

7.1 The File Tab/Backstage View

If you are familiar with versions of Word earlier than 2007, you will likely be happy to once again see the File Tab in Word versions 2013 and later. In the 2007 version, Microsoft replaced the File menu with the "Backstage" area or "Office Button." This caused a lot of confusion among users. Microsoft had spent decades teaching us to use the File menu with previous versions – then it was suddenly gone. The File Tab leverages our original training by putting many of the same options under the File Tab as we were used to seeing under the File menu. Let's take a look at each of the links on the File Tab. (Note that to exit the File Tab and return to the actual document (e.g., for additional writing or editing), click the arrow at the top.)

Figure 36: Backstage view

The Backstage View is the central managing place for all Word documents. To go to the backstage of the Word document, click on the **File** tab in the **Ribbon** Tabs bar.

You can create, save, open, print, or share your document from backstage. Starting from the top, the:

- **New** allows you to open a new Word document.

- **Open** allows you to open the document you created earlier from different locations.

- **Info** gives information about the Word document, allowing you to protect, inspect and manage your document.

- **Save** saves the current document with the same name and location.

- **Save as** will enable you to rename, select the desired location and save the recent document.

- **Print** allows you to print your document in the desired format.

- **Share** lets you share your document through email or online.

- **Export** allows you to create the PDF or XPS document of your Word document.

- **Account** contains all the document holder's details. You can change the look of your Office applications and do some other settings here.

- **Close** allows you to exit the current document. The Top-left-corner **arrow** will enable you to go back to the document area.

- **Options** opens the **Word Options** dialog box

Info

Document Properties

Take a look at the following image. The Info link on the File Tab shows us several of the document's properties, including Size, Pages, Number of Words, Create/Modify Times, etc. Also, notice the "Show All Properties" link at the bottom.

Figure 37: Info Backstage

Document properties, as you may suspect, contain information about the document. These properties have gained significant attention in recent years due to privacy concerns. Some of these properties are editable, while others are automatically calculated. Some are accessible via the "File" Tab (see the previous image), while others are embedded in the document and only accessible via special editing techniques or software tools. In any case, be aware of their existence, usefulness, and potential privacy implications.

New

This link displays a gallery of available document templates. When you click on a template, a new document is created using that template.

Save / Save As

As the names imply, these links save the document, with "Save As" prompting you for a new document name or type first. We recommend creating QAT buttons for these instead. That's faster and easier than using the File Tab for a simple save operation.

Compatibility: Saving As

Windows, MAC, Android, iPads, OpenOffice, LibreOffice…

There are so many more document editing platforms than there used to be – or, at least, it seems like there are. Unfortunately, more platforms mean more compatibility issues. Let's look at how we can address some of those issues by saving our document as an alternate file type.

File Types

Figure 38: Save file extension types

-DOCX: Word's native file type.

-DOC: Save in this format if you intend to share this file with someone with a pre-2007 version of MS Office. This format is also helpful for some non-Microsoft-based document editors. Be careful, though. You could lose some of your data or formatting when saving in this format.

Note: Don't forget to recommend the Compatibility Pack to those who use MS Office 2003.

-RTF: Many non-Microsoft document editors can read this format. The downside of this format is that its resulting file sizes can become much larger. DOC files with the same content. Thus, sharing these files can become more complex.

- TXT: Use this format if you want Word to strip out all of the formatting from the document leaving only the text. Caution, your document will not look the same.

- PDF: The .PDF format is native to the Adobe Acrobat software application. It's generally considered a good format for sharing your document with others as long as they will not need to edit it. However, once in PDF format, you will be very limited in your ability to edit the document.

- HTML file: The HTML format is read by Internet browsers such as Internet Explorer or Safari. Almost all modern computers will be able to read this format (via an installed browser application), but the editing capabilities are much more limited than the .DOCX format.

Print

This link does two things for us:

-Provides options for printing

-Provides a Print Preview.

As with the Save link, we recommend just creating a QAT button for this.

Share

The "Share" option has been around for many years, but previously, it was focused primarily on sharing via email. Word gives us a few additional options.

Export

Honestly, we are not quite sure why there is a need for the Export link. You can accomplish the same thing with the Save As link.

Figure 39: Export option on backstage

Close

Easy explanation here: This link closes your current document. It also prompts you to save the document if any changes have been made since you opened it.

Account

You probably won't spend much time with this link if you are not using OneDrive or any other Microsoft online services. However, if you use any Microsoft services, they will be listed, and any configurable options will be presented.

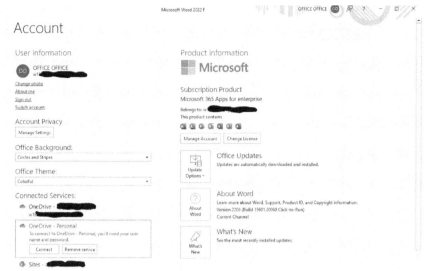

Figure 40: Account option on backstage

Options

Remember the Good ol' Days when you could click on "Tools" in the menu and select "Options?" Well, those days are gone, but the Options live on. The image below shows the Options window with its many, well, options.

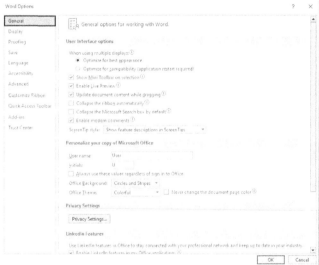

Figure 41: Options on backstage

General

The only thing we ever change on this Tab is the Office Theme. To us, the White option looks too washed out and makes the Word window too difficult to distinguish from any other windows you may have open. We use the "Colorful."

Display

Nothing much of interest for us there.

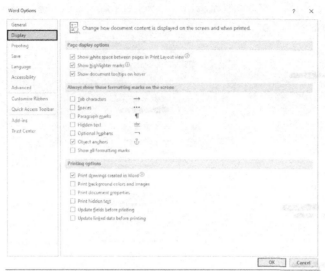

Figure 42: Options Display on backstage

Proofing

Here is where you can tweak your Spellcheck and Grammar options. The following image shows our typical settings; your preferences may vary.

Notice the "Show Readability Statistics" option. More about that feature later.

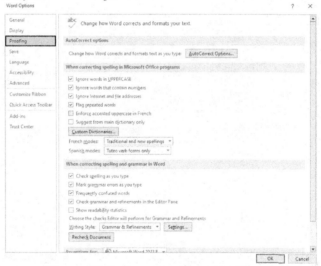

Figure 43: Options Proofing on backstage

Save

Perhaps it has happened to you: You were working on a **large** document in Word, suddenly Word crashes, and your document is gone, or perhaps you forgot to save your changes before closing Word. The information in the Save options may help you keep your sanity. This information includes:

-Where to find "Autosaved" documents (that is, drafts that Word automatically saves as you are working on a Word document)

-How often Word Autosaves our work. Consider whether the default of every 10 minutes is appropriate for you.

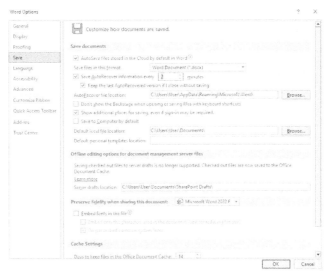

Figure 44: Options Save on backstage

Language & Advanced

We typically don't have much interest in either of these two links. The defaults tend to work well for us. Check them out for yourself, though.

Customize Ribbon & Quick Access Toolbar

Here are a couple of links with which we highly recommend you spend some time. Customizing the Ribbon may seem daunting due to all the options, but it could be well worth your time investment. Do away with the command buttons you don't use in the Ribbon and replace them with the command buttons you will use. The same goes for the QAT (Quick Access Toolbar). See our previous discussion on the QAT for our recommendations.

Add-Ins

You're probably only visiting this page if you have an Add-In problem. Add-Ins are pieces of software that extend the functionality of the native Word application.

A note about Add-Ins: having too many enabled can slow down Word's performance.

Trust Center

Chances are you won't be spending too much time here either. If you spend time here, it will probably be within the Trust Center Settings button.

If you've used Word 2010 or later for any length of time, you've probably encountered the "Enable Content" or "Enable Editing" prompt at the top of the edit pane.

This prompt appears when you open a document from a source that Word does not "Trust." You can tell Word to trust sources using the Trust Center Settings, and more specifically, Trusted Publishers, Trusted Locations, and Trusted Documents.

The final item within the Trust Center Settings: Privacy Options. Check these out for yourself to make sure they match your privacy expectations. The "Document Inspector" feature is related to the privacy options you may wish to become familiar with.

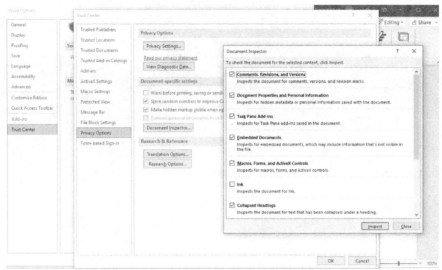

Figure 45: Document inspector

That's a wrap on our File tab discussion. Now let's talk about some of Word's document editing and content-related features.

DOCUMENT AREA

Page

The page is the white window where all your input will be displayed. There is always a vertical blinking line on the page called **insertion point**. The insertion point indicates where text or anything you put into your document will be added. You can relocate your insertion point to the desired place by moving your cursor and double-clicking in the area.

When printed, your document will appear in the paper exactly how it appears on the page.

Scroll Bars

There are two scroll bars in the Word document area, the vertical and horizontal scroll bars. The vertical scroll bar allows you to scroll your document downward and upward, while the horizontal scroll bar will enable you to scroll your document left and right. The scroll bars only appear if all the document pages cannot be displayed on the window.

To scroll your document page, left-click on the scroll bar, hold and drag down, up, left, or right as the case may be. You can also left-click on the arrows at the terminals of the scroll bar, hold down for fast movement and click intermittently for slow movement.

Rulers

Word has two rulers; a vertical and a horizontal ruler. The horizontal ruler is used for quick indent settings (to be discussed in full later).

STATUS BAR

The status bar contains specific information about the Word document or selected text. The status bar default contains the current page, total page numbers, word counts, language, zoom slider, and page view icons.

Zoom Bar

- This bar allows you to zoom in and out of the document to make your document page appears larger and smaller, respectively, as desired.

- Drag the slider either towards the right side (+) or left side (-) to zoom in and out, respectively. You can also click on the bar to position the slider.

- Click on + and – to increase or reduce the view with multiples of 10.

- Click on the percentage tab to open the zoom window to set the page view.

- You can only set the zoom between 10% and 500%.

8 PAGE DIMENSION AND MARGINS

Page dimension refers to the width and height of a page. You can make your document's page dimensions match the paper's size or have them follow a specific pattern. Margins refer to the space on a page's top/bottom and sides. Again, you can increase or decrease them to make your document look precisely as you want. Page margins in Word are the spaces between your body text and the page edge. You can use these areas for headers and footers. The margins are a critical part of making your document readable. A generous margin will make your text look inviting, while a narrow margin will give reviewers enough space to write their comments. Too many words per line and long lines will make reading your document difficult. Page margins are significant for documents with many pages or facing pages. Word provides several predefined margins, including one inch on all sides. A 1-inch margin is the default setting, but you can change it to fit your needs. If you need a smaller margin, click the "Normal" button on the Page Setup dialog box, then select "Custom Margins." This dialog box will allow you to set the top and bottom margins separately. You can also change the margins individually for the left and right sides. There are many page layout options in Microsoft Word. For example, you can customize the width of your document, its orientation, and the margins. There are also options to control the spacing of text and images. You can choose one of these options based on the document you're working on.

Margins and Making Adjustments

In MS Word, as well as the older versions of the same application, margins are blank spaces that line your document's left, right, top, and bottom. When you type text in your document, the text does not cut into those margins. They are boundaries that your words cannot break into.

There are default margin sizes assigned for each document type chosen. In the field of books and script publications, there are standards that the manuscript's owner must maintain before his work is accepted. For instance, you have written a book in A4 Word document and then want to send it to a publishing firm for them to print it as a book for you. The publishing firm may inform you to format your manuscript in a particular margin size before they accept your work. That is a standard. So, let me walk you through how you can get to the margin section and then make the changes you need.

To access the margin of your Word document, click on the *Layout* tab of your document. When you do that, you will see some commands, one of which is *Margins*. Click on the **Margins** command to see some options in the photo below.

Figure 46: The options for Margins command

You will see the margins size of your document. On the other hand, you can select another new margin to form the list. There are options like *narrow, moderate, mirrored,* and the rest.

You can insert new margins if you do not want to select from the margins list. Select the Custom Margins option as you click on the Margins command to achieve that. When you do that, a dialog box will open. Type the margin sizes you want in the spaces provided for you.

Columns of Word Document and Adjustments

Just like the way you can access margin sizes, as explained in the previous subheading, you can access the column sizes of your Word document and choose something different for yourself. It is simple to do, and when you select a column different from the one assigned to your document by default, you will see the impact on your document. To access the column of your Word document or make changes to it, tap on the *Layout* tab, followed by *columns*. This action will display some options. Click on the column you want your document to be formatted in. As you do that, you will see how it will change the layout of your document immediately.

9 TIPS AND TRICKS FOR FORMATTING AND EDITING

What is style formatting in Microsoft Word?

Style formatting is a way to neatly format text using one of the styles available in Word. Styles are sets of formatting instructions that can be used for different text types. To create a style, select all the text you want to use, choose Home, Styles, and type in the Style Name. Next, select Change Style and choose New or Copy to copy your selected text. Next, choose Home again and click the Close button in the upper right corner.

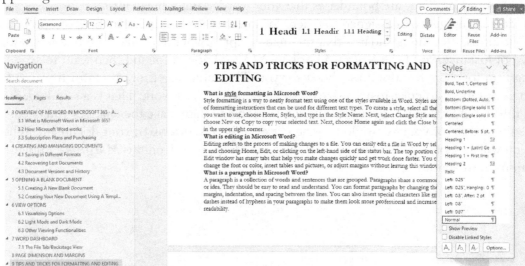

Figure 47: Styles under Home tab

What is editing in Microsoft Word?

Editing refers to the process of making changes to a file. You can easily edit a file in Word by selecting it and choosing Home, Edit, or clicking on the left-hand side of the status bar. The top portion of the Edit window has many tabs that help you make changes quickly and get work done faster. You can change the font or color, insert tables and pictures, or adjust margins without leaving this window.

What is a paragraph in Microsoft Word?

A paragraph is a collection of words and sentences that are grouped. Paragraphs share a common topic or idea. They should be easy to read and understand. You can format paragraphs by changing the size, margins, indentation, and spacing between the lines. You can also insert special characters like em dashes instead of hyphens in your paragraphs to make them look more professional and increase their readability.

What is a font in Microsoft Word?

A font is a collection of character shapes and sizes. Many different fonts are available in Word, including serifs, sans-serifs, and fancy letter styles. You can use several of them simultaneously to make your document look more interesting. According to Microsoft, fonts define a certain style of the text.

What is the font size in Microsoft Word?

Text size refers to the size of the letters in a font. Font sizes are usually measured in points, which can be confusing. For example, the 10-point text is usually smaller than 12 point text. The higher the number, the larger your font will be. You can use dozens of fonts and sizes to make different sections of your document look as professional as possible or add visual interest.

What is font formatting?

Font formatting refers to changing the appearance of your selected text in Microsoft Word. For example, you can make your text bold, italic, underlined, or strikethrough by choosing a font style from the Home tab.

What is letter spacing in Microsoft Word?

Letter spacing measures how far apart letters are in a font. You can increase or decrease the space between letters by turning on or off character spacing, which will cause the letter to draw closer together. This can make your document look more professional.

What is font color in Microsoft Word?

Font color refers to the colors that appear in a font. You can set the colors of your font by choosing one from a black and white drop-down menu on the home tab. You can also apply gradients for more design options, but these will not appear on printed versions of your document.

What is the font color behind the text in Microsoft Word?

Font color behind text refers to the ability to change the color of all or part of the text in your selected paragraph, so it appears behind text from other paragraphs. This can make your document look more professional by giving the impression that you are sending a written message.

What are uppercase and lowercase in Microsoft Word?

Uppercase letters are normally printed using capital letters, but some words can use uppercase letters or other characters. Uppercasing is the process of converting all lowercase letters to capital form. Lowercase letters are normally printed using small letters, but some words can use lowercase or other characters. Lowercasing is the process of converting all uppercase letters to a lowercase form. Word automatically makes your entire document use uppercase or lowercase, but you can change this feature by selecting which type of text you want.

How to add new fonts in Microsoft Word?

Go to the Home tab and choose Fonts and Text. From the drop-down menu that appears, choose Add New Font. Type in the Name of your font, Click the "Browse" button to find the font from your computer. Print screen this page to see the font on your screen. Find the font you want on your computer and print screen it. Click the OK button to add a new font in Microsoft Word for Windows. Place it under the All fonts option in the Home tab - More Fonts option of Microsoft Word for Windows.

What's compare mode and combine mode in Microsoft Word?

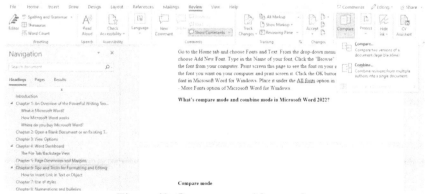

Figure 48: Compare combine modes

Compare mode

This function lets you compare two windows side by side. When you click on the 'Compare' button, the right window with the cursor moves over to the left window, and then after some time, it switches back to the original.

Combine mode

In this case, you hold the Shift key while clicking on the 'Compare' button. In this way, both windows are combined into one. After holding down the Shift key, click on Compare button again and select 'Merge.' This combination occurs only when you hold down the Shift key.

9.1 Advanced Word Settings

Customize your Word experience with advanced settings for editing, display, printing, and more. To access these settings, go to File > Options > Advanced.

Editing: Adjust how you select, format, and replace text.

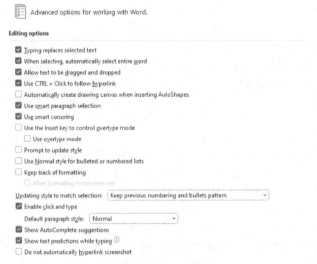

Figure 49: Editing Options

Cut/Copy/Paste: Set preferences for copying and pasting within or across documents.

Cut, copy, and paste

Pasting within the same document:	Keep Source Formatting (Default) ⌄
Pasting between documents:	Keep Source Formatting (Default) ⌄
Pasting between documents when style definitions conflict:	Use Destination Styles (Default) ⌄
Pasting from other programs:	Keep Source Formatting (Default) ⌄
Insert/paste pictures as:	In line with text ⌄

☑ Keep bullets and numbers when pasting text with Keep Text Only option

☐ Use the Insert key for paste

☑ Show Paste Options button when content is pasted

☑ Use smart cut and paste ① [Settings...]

Figure 50: Cut, copy, and paste

Image Settings: Adjust image quality and size for the current or new documents.

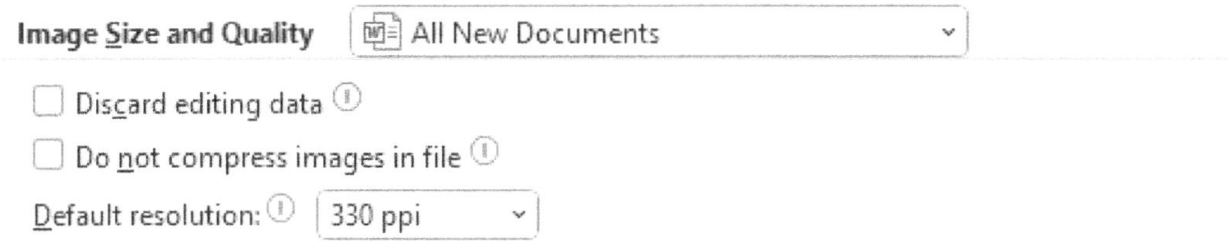

Image Size and Quality | 📄 All New Documents ⌄

☐ Discard editing data ⓘ
☐ Do not compress images in file ⓘ
Default resolution: ⓘ | 330 ppi ⌄

Figure 51: Image Size and Quality

Charts: Keep custom labels and formatting consistent, even if the chart alters.

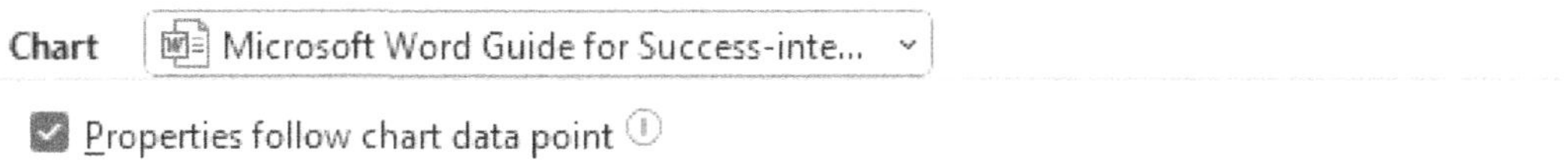

Chart | 📄 Microsoft Word Guide for Success-inte... ⌄

☑ Properties follow chart data point ⓘ

Figure 52: Chart

Content Display: Set preferences for how text, images, and formatting appear.

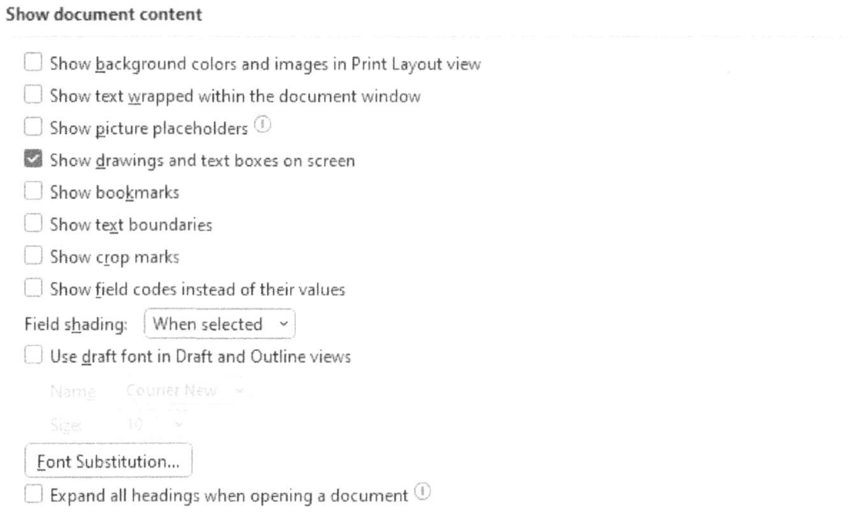

Show document content

☐ Show background colors and images in Print Layout view
☐ Show text wrapped within the document window
☐ Show picture placeholders ⓘ
☑ Show drawings and text boxes on screen
☐ Show bookmarks
☐ Show text boundaries
☐ Show crop marks
☐ Show field codes instead of their values
Field shading: | When selected ⌄
☐ Use draft font in Draft and Outline views
　　Name　Courier New ⌄
　　Size　10 ⌄
[Font Substitution...]
☐ Expand all headings when opening a document ⓘ

Figure 53: Displaying document content

Display Settings: Set measurement units, show scroll bars, and manage the 'Recent Documents' list.

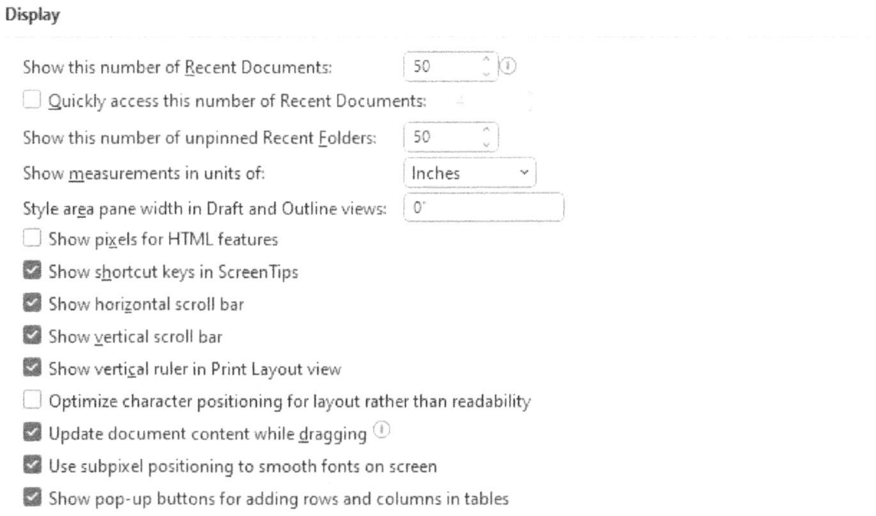

Display

Show this number of Recent Documents: | 50 | ⓘ
☐ Quickly access this number of Recent Documents:
Show this number of unpinned Recent Folders: | 50
Show measurements in units of: | Inches ⌄
Style area pane width in Draft and Outline views: | 0"
☐ Show pixels for HTML features
☑ Show shortcut keys in ScreenTips
☑ Show horizontal scroll bar
☑ Show vertical scroll bar
☑ Show vertical ruler in Print Layout view
☐ Optimize character positioning for layout rather than readability
☑ Update document content while dragging ⓘ
☑ Use subpixel positioning to smooth fonts on screen
☑ Show pop-up buttons for adding rows and columns in tables

Figure 54: The display settings

Printing: Adjust settings for print appearance and paper size.

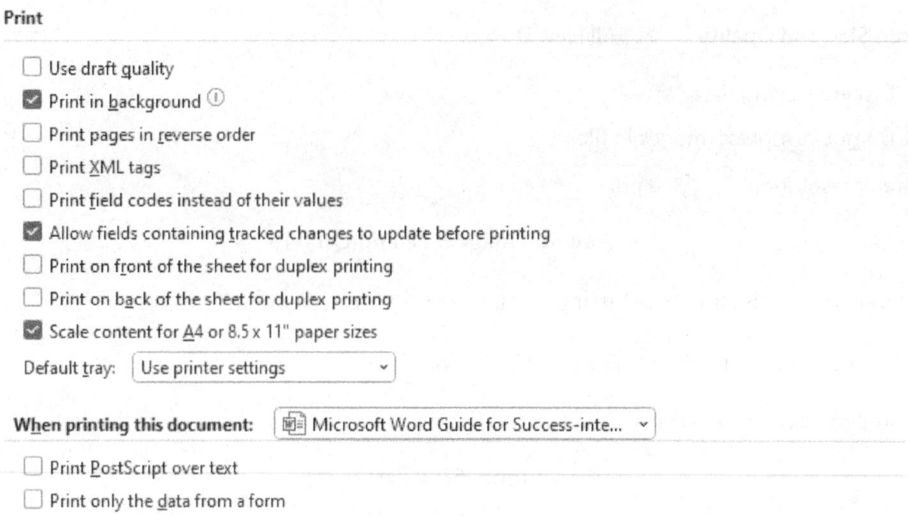

Print

☐ Use draft quality
☑ Print in background ⓘ
☐ Print pages in reverse order
☐ Print XML tags
☐ Print field codes instead of their values
☑ Allow fields containing tracked changes to update before printing
☐ Print on front of the sheet for duplex printing
☐ Print on back of the sheet for duplex printing
☑ Scale content for A4 or 8.5 x 11" paper sizes
Default tray: Use printer settings ▾

When printing this document: [W] Microsoft Word Guide for Success-inte... ▾

☐ Print PostScript over text
☐ Print only the data from a form

Figure 55: The Print settings

Saving: Set auto-save options, backup preferences, and template saving settings.

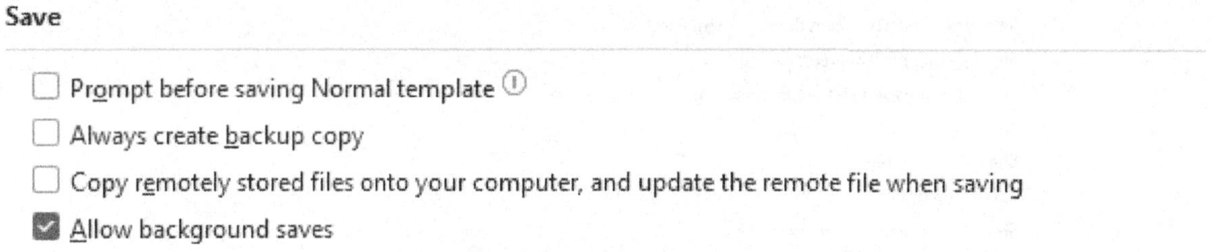

Save

☐ Prompt before saving Normal template ⓘ
☐ Always create backup copy
☐ Copy remotely stored files onto your computer, and update the remote file when saving
☑ Allow background saves

Figure 56: Settings for Save

Document Sharing: Ensure your document's appearance remains consistent when shared with users of different Word versions.

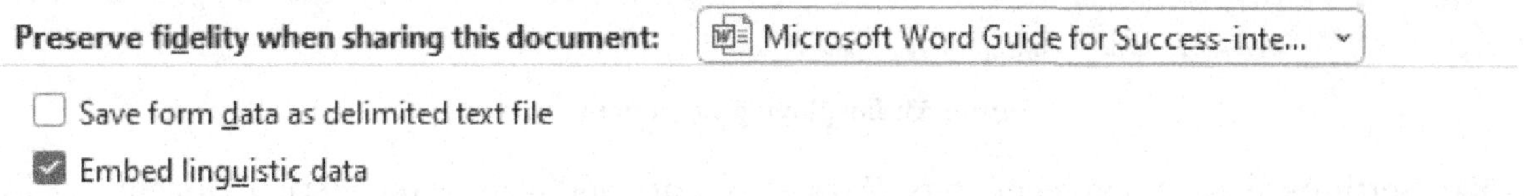

Preserve fidelity when sharing this document: [W] Microsoft Word Guide for Success-inte... ▾

☐ Save form data as delimited text file
☑ Embed linguistic data

Figure 57: Sharing the document

General: Change default save locations or open documents in a specific view.

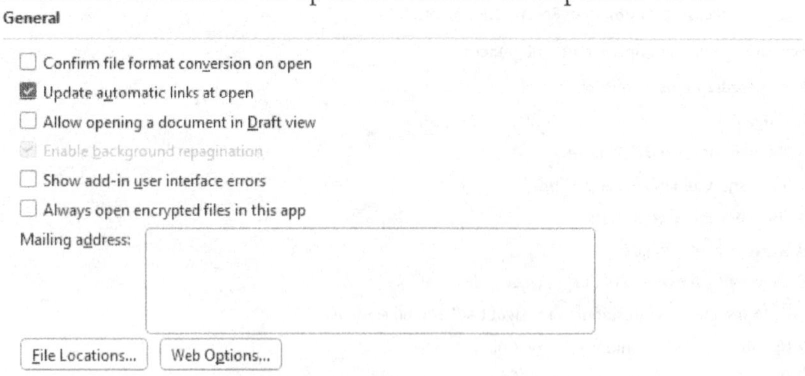

General

☐ Confirm file format conversion on open
☑ Update automatic links at open
☐ Allow opening a document in Draft view
☑ Enable background repagination
☐ Show add-in user interface errors
☐ Always open encrypted files in this app
Mailing address:

[File Locations...] [Web Options...]

Figure 58: Settings for general

Layout: Adjust layout settings like character spacing for the current or future documents.

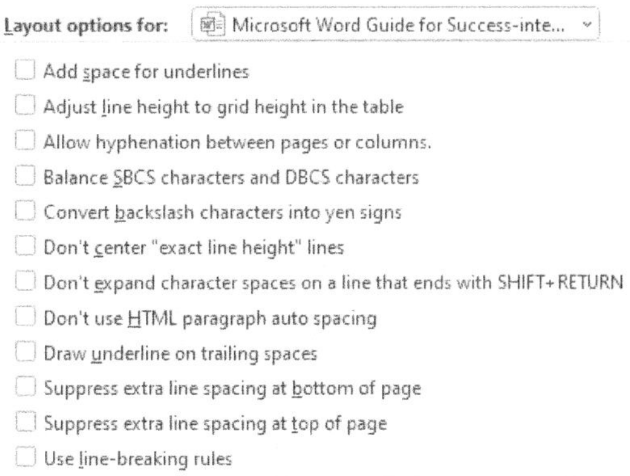

```
Layout options for:   [📄] Microsoft Word Guide for Success-inte...  ▾

☐ Add space for underlines
☐ Adjust line height to grid height in the table
☐ Allow hyphenation between pages or columns.
☐ Balance SBCS characters and DBCS characters
☐ Convert backslash characters into yen signs
☐ Don't center "exact line height" lines
☐ Don't expand character spaces on a line that ends with SHIFT+RETURN
☐ Don't use HTML paragraph auto spacing
☐ Draw underline on trailing spaces
☐ Suppress extra line spacing at bottom of page
☐ Suppress extra line spacing at top of page
☐ Use line-breaking rules
```

Figure 59: Layout options

ENTERING, SELECTING, AND DELETING TEXTS

To Enter Texts into your Document:

1. Open your MS Word
2. Pick a blank document, a template, or an existing document. Word automatically sets the text insertion point at the top of the first page of any newly opened document.
3. For existing documents: Scroll down and click the point you want to enter new texts, like the last page, to reposition the insertion point.
4. Type your new texts on the keyboard, and the texts will appear at the text insertion point.

Note:

- Press the space bar using your keyboard once to put space between words.
- Do not Press **Enter** button to move to the following line. Word automatically moves to the next line when the current line is filled.
- Press the Enter button on your keyboard only when starting a new paragraph.
- Word automatically creates a new page once the current one is filled.

To Select Texts in MS Word:

1. Put your cursor on the texts you want to pick.
2. Left-click your mouse, holding it down, and move it across the texts.
3. Release the mouse.

OR

1. Click at the start of the texts you want to select.
2. Hold down the **Shift** button using your keyboard
3. Click at the end of the texts or **press** any arrow keys on your keyboard to select the texts in the direction of the arrow.

Some Shortcut ways of selecting Texts:

To select:

- **A word** – Double-click on the word.
- **A line** – Place the mouse pointer at the left margin and click **once** in front of the line.
- **A sentence** – Press and hold the **Ctrl** button on your keyboard, then click anywhere on the sentence.
- **A paragraph** – Place the mouse pointer in the left margin and double-click next to any paragraph line. You can Triple-click anywhere in the paragraph.
- **The whole Document** – Press the **Ctrl** key, place your mouse pointer anywhere in the margin, and triple-click or left-click once anywhere in the margin. Alternatively,

- Go to the **Home** tab, click on **Select** in **Editing** group, and **select all. OR**
- Press **Ctrl + A** on your keyboard.

To Select several texts that are not together:
Press down the **Ctrl** button and use any of the methods stated above to select the texts one after the other.

To Delete Texts:
1. Highlight the texts you want to delete.
2. Press the **Delete** button on your keyboard

OR
1. Move your cursor to the left side of the text you wish to delete.
2. Press the **Delete** button on your keyboard.

OR
1. Move your cursor to the right of the texts you want to delete
2. Press the **Backspace** button on your keyboard.

Deleting a Single Character
You can use the keyboard to add and remove text when you write in Word. Many keys make text, but Backspace and Delete are the only keys that can delete text. These keys become more powerful when used with other keys, or even the mouse, that help them delete large amounts of text.

- **The Delete key** deletes characters to the **right** of the insertion pointer

- **The backspace key** deletes characters to the **left** of the insertion pointer.

Deleting a Word
You can delete an entire world with the Ctrl, Backspace, or Delete keys. There are two ways to use these keyboard shortcuts. They work best when the insertion pointer is at the start or end of a word. Delete commands are only used when the pointer is in the middle of a word. These commands only delete from that middle point to the start or end of the word. The shortcut to delete is illustrated as follows;

- The word to the left of the insertion pointer is deleted when you press **Ctrl+Backspace.**

- The word to the right of the insertion pointer is deleted when you press **Ctrl + Delete.**

Note: When you use Ctrl+Backspace, delete a word to the left. The pointer is at the end of what comes before it. When you use Ctrl+Delete to remove a word, the cursor moves to the start of the next word. This is done to make removing several words in a row easier.

Deleting More Than a Word
The keyboard and mouse must work together to remove chunks of text bigger than a single letter or word. The first step is to choose a chunk of text and then delete that chunk text.

Remove a Line of Text
A line of text starts on one side of the page and goes to the other. If you want to remove the line, you can:

- Make sure the mouse pointer is next to a line of text by moving it to the left.

- Then click on the mouse.

- The text line is chosen and shown in a different color on the screen.

- Press the delete key to delete that line.

Delete a Sentence
A sentence is a group of text made up of words that start with a capital letter and end with a period, a question mark, or an exclamation point, depending on what you want to say. To do this;

- Place the mouse pointer where the sentence you want to delete lies.

- Press and hold down the Ctrl key simultaneously as you click the mouse.

- Using Ctrl and a mouse click together, you can choose a sentence of text that you want to delete.

- The Ctrl key can be let go, and then you can hit delete.

Deleting a Paragraph

A Paragraph is a group of sentences formed when you press the Enter key. If you want to delete a whole paragraph quickly, here's how to do it:

- Click the mouse **three times.** In this case, the triple-click selects the whole paragraph of the text.

- Press the **Delete button.**

Another way to select a paragraph is to click the mouse two times in the left margin, next to the paragraph, to make it select and then click on delete.

Deleting a Page

Page of text is everything on a page from top to bottom. This part of the document isn't one that Word directly addresses with keyboard commands. You'll need some sleight of hand to get rid of a whole page of text. Take these steps:

- Press the keys **Ctrl+G.**

- The Find and Replace dialogue box comes up, with the Go To tab at the top of the list of tabs.

- On the Go to What list, choose Page and then type the number of the page you want to remove.

- Click the Go To button, then the Close button. And the page shows up.

- Press the **Delete** button.

- All of the text on the page is taken off.

Split and Join Paragraphs

A paragraph, as earlier defined, is a group of sentences that all say the same thing about a thought, idea, or theme. In Word, a paragraph is a chunk of text that ends when you press the Enter key. You can change a paragraph in a document by splitting or joining text.

To split a single paragraph in two;

When you want to start a new paragraph, click the mouse where you want it to start. That point should be at the beginning of a sentence. Press the Enter button. During this process, Word breaks the paragraph in two. The text above the insertion pointer becomes its paragraph, and the text below becomes the next paragraph.

Making a single paragraph out of two separate ones

To combine two paragraphs and make them one, do this; When you place the insertion pointer at the start of the second paragraph or use the keyboard or click the mouse to move the insertion pointer where you want it to be, press the Backspace button.

This implies that you have removed the entered character from the paragraph before this one, thus making two paragraphs into one.

Soft and Hard Return

The **Return or Enter key** is pressed at the end of each line when typing on a keyboard. This indicates that you've finished one paragraph and are ready to go on to the next. However, when you set your page margins, Word knows that your text should wrap to the next line when you get to the right margin. However, there may be situations when you want to stop writing a line before reaching the right margin. You can terminate a line in one of two ways in these circumstances. The first method is to enter where you want the line to terminate and then hit Enter. As a result, the document is filled with a **hard return.** This action (hitting Enter) signifies that you have reached the end of the paragraph and wish to begin a new one. Another approach to end a line is to hit **Shift+Enter,** which will insert a soft return, also known as a line break or newline character, into the document. The end of a paragraph is indicated by hard returns, whereas soft returns indicate the end of a line**.**

A hard return displays on your screen as a paragraph mark (a backward P), while a soft return appears as a down-and-left pointing arrow.

To replace texts:

1. Select the texts.

2. Type the new texts over it.

You do not need to delete the texts; Word automatically deletes the old selected texts and replaces them with the newly typed text.

CUT, COPY AND PASTE TEXTS

Cutting text removes the text from its initial position and places it where it is **Pasted** while **copying** reproduces the text in another place.

There are various ways of copying, cutting, and pasting texts in Word; some of the top ones include the following:

Method 1:

- Pick the text you want to cut or copy.

- Click on the **Home** tab and select the Copy or Cut command as desired.

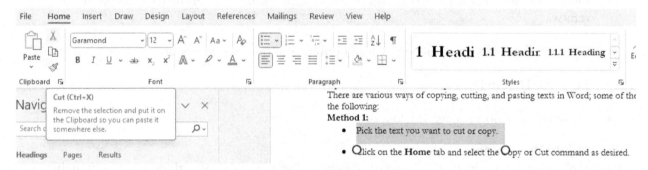

Figure 60: Home tab copy cut

- Put your cursor to where you want to paste your text.

- Click on the **Paste** command in the **Home** tab.

Method 2:

- Select the texts you want to copy or cut.

- Right-click on the selected text.

Figure 61: Right click copy cut

- Select the **Copy** or **Cut** option from the menu that appears.

- Place your cursor to the desired location and right-click on your mouse.

- Select the **Paste** option with a left-click from a menu that appears.

Alternatively, you can use the shortcut commands:
- **Ctrl + C** to copy

- **Ctrl + X** to cut

- **Ctrl + V** or **Shift + Insert** to paste

Tips: You can use the **paste** option to paste the item you copied or cut last as many times and at many places as desired.

9.2 Paste Special Options And Clipboard

Paste Special Options
While working on your document, you will likely want to copy/cut some texts that already have formatting, like font type, font size, color, etc. When you copy/cut these formatted texts into word, Word automatically reformats the texts to the destination format, which might not be what you want. However, depending on your choice, Paste Special Option is provided to help you retain the original format and paste the item as a link, picture, or plain text.
Paste Special is a word feature that provides several format options to Paste your item. The format in which you can paste your texts includes Microsoft Word Object, Formatted text, Unformatted text, Picture, file, Html format, and Unformatted Unicode Text (UUT).
To use Paste Special Options:
- Copy or cut the item you want to paste, e.g., text, picture, shape, slide, etc.
- Click where you want to insert the item in your document.
- Go to the **Home** tab in the **Clipboard** group and click the dropdown arrow under **Paste.**
- Select **Paste Special** from the menu that comes up.

Figure 62: Paste special

- Choose one of the options from the pop-up window as desired.

Alternatively, you can use the **Ctrl + Alt + V** shortcut command on your keyboard to call the **Paste Special** window.

Note: The **Paste Special** options change based on the item you want to paste.

Clipboard

A clipboard is a location where the cut or copy texts are temporarily stored and can be recalled for use with a **Paste** command. Microsoft has a multi-clipboard that can store up to 24 items copied or cut, unlike a window clipboard that can only hold one item at a time. The **Paste** command only recalls the last item copied or cut, and you can assess the other items by opening the clipboard.

To paste any of your copied items from the clipboard:

1. Go to **the Home** tab, under the **clipboard** group.
2. Click the expandable dialog box button to display the clipboard with the list of all the copied/cut items.

Figure 63: Clipboard paste

3. Click on the item of your choice to paste it at the insertion point or
4. Move your cursor to the item you want, and in front, you will see a drop-down button with options to paste or delete.

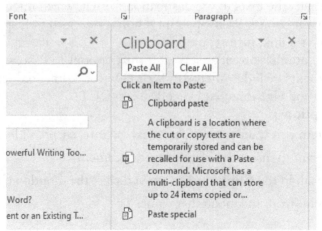

Figure 64: Items on clipboard

5. Select **Paste**, and your item will be inserted into the insertion point. **Delete** and remove the data from the clipboard if you do not need it again.

Click the **x** button to close the clipboard panel and **arrow** down options to change its location (move), resize, or close it as desired.

MOVING AND DUPLICATING

Moving removes the text or object from its initial position to another location, just like cut and paste, while duplicating reproduces your text in another place like copy and paste. It is easier to move/duplicate than cut/copy and paste.

The difference between Cut/copy, and move/duplicate is that while cut/copy stores their items in the clipboard, move/duplicate never does. Therefore, using the cut/copy and paste command is advisable if you need the item later because you can easily retrieve them on the clipboard.

To move your text:

- Select the texts or items you want to move.

- Click and hold your mouse

- drag and drop the item in the desired location.

To duplicate your text:

- Select the item you want to duplicate.

- Click and hold your mouse on the item.

- Press and hold down the **Ctrl** key.

- Drag and **drop** the item in the desired location.

- Then release the **Ctrl** button last.

Note: If you release the **Ctrl** button before releasing the item in the new location, the item will be moved and not duplicated.

UNDO, REDO, AND REPEAT

MS Word keeps track of most of your tasks while working on your document until you close the document. You can undo tasks like formatting, typing, deleting, etc., and some actions like clicking on a command, saving your document, etc., you cannot undo. By default, Word can save up to **100** tasks you can undo.

To redo a task only a step back;

- Click on the undo icon in the **Quick Access Toolbar** once

- or even more for more steps backward.

For many steps backward;

- Click on the dropdown button in front of the undo icon;

- a list of all the tasks you have performed since you open the document up to 100 appears.

- Select a point in the list, and Word will undo everything you have done. You can only undo all the steps from the present to a point you select on the list. You cannot undo a single action that is not immediate.

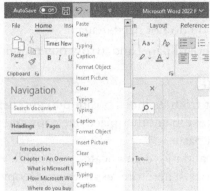

Figure 65: Undo actions

If you do not want to undo your task again, the redo command [icon] is also available for you to use in the **Quick Access Toolbar**. If there is nothing to redo, Words change the redo icon to repeat icon [icon] for you to repeat some repeatable actions.

The redo and undo action command becomes inactive if there is nothing to undo or redo.

<u>Keyboard Shortcuts:</u>

Press **Ctrl + Z to undo.**

Press **Ctrl + Y to redo or repeat** as the case may be.

The Undo Command

The Undo command can undo anything you do in Word, like changing text, moving blocks, typing, and deleting text. It does this for everything you do in the program. If you want to use the Undo command, you have two ways to do it:

- The shortcut method is to Press **Ctrl+Z.**

- Alternatively, you can click the Undo command button on the Quick Access toolbar to get back to where your previous work is.

Note: In some cases, you can't use the Undo command because there's nothing to undo. For example, you can't go back and undo a file save.

The Redo Command

If you make a mistake and undo something you didn't mean to, use the Redo command to get things back to how they used to be. Suppose you write some text and then use Undo to remove the text. Then, you can use the Redo command to go back and type again. It's your choice. You can choose

- The shortcut method is to press **Ctrl+Y.**

- Alternatively, look at the **Quick Access toolbar** and click the **Redo button.**

Note: The Undo command does the opposite of the Redo command. So, if you write text, Undo removes the text, and Redo puts the text back.

The Repeat Command

To repeat what you did in Word last time, use the Repeat command to do the same thing again. This could be typing new text, formatting it, or doing many other things.

Using the Repeat command, you can keep the same picture. The Redo command turns into the Repeat command whenever there is no more to redo.

To do this:

- The shortcut method is to Press **Ctrl+Y**, which is the same keyboard shortcut as to redo something.

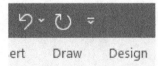

Figure 66: The Undo and Repeat Button

Finally, now that you know how to use the basic tools in Word to make a document, this chapter has covered some more editing tools and simple formatting effects to make a document look better. More editing tools will be discussed in other chapters.

9.3 How to Insert Link in Text or Object

I do not know your area of specialization as the reader of this book or what area you want to go into in the future. But whatever the area, I believe no knowledge is a waste. For example, in online writing (blogging), we embed links in texts and sometimes photos. When readers click on the text or photos having these links they cannot see, they are taken to a specific website. So, I will teach you how to insert links in text or photos in a Word document. To insert the link in a text or photo, the first step you are to take is to select the text or photo. If you want to insert the link in a text, get the text selected. If you do the insertion in a photo you have in your Word document, select the photo by clicking on it once. The next step you are to take after the selection is to click on the **Insert** tab of your Word document. Click on the dropdown at the **Link** icon indicated in the photo below.

Figure 67: The Link icon

The Insert Link dialog box will open on your computer. In the **Address** space, type the link you want to connect to, for example, www.amazon.com. And then tap on the **OK** button. This last step will hyperlink the text or image you selected. Anytime a reader clicks on that text. They will be taken to the website whenever a link is added in a text, and the text color changes, usually blue, by default. Hyperlinking a text turns the text into a link and makes it clickable. The link, when clicked, jumps to another location, either in the document or a different location outside the document, like a website, another file, a new email message, or any other place the text is being hyperlinked to. This feature is excellent for easy navigation of your document.

MS word automatically convert a web address to a hyperlink when you type the address and press **Enter** or **Spacebar** after the address, e.g., www.office.com

To turn your text into a Hyperlink:

1. Select the text you want to turn to a link.
2. Go to the **Insert** tab under the **Links** group. You can also right-click on the text: A menu appears.
3. Click the **Link** command.
4. Select the link destination and fill in the required information in the **Insert Hyperlink** window. There are four available options to choose from based on what you want:

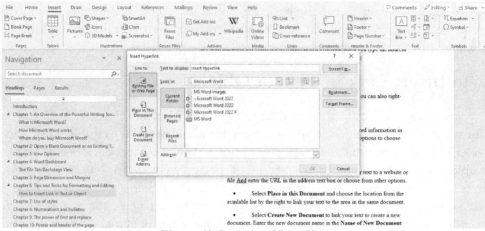

Figure 68: Inserting Hyperlink

- Select **Existing File or Web Page** to link your text to a website or file And enter the URL in the address text box or choose from other options.

- Select **Place in this Document** and choose the location from the available list by the right to link your text to the area in the same document.

- Select **Create New Document** to link your text to create a new document. Enter the new document name in the **Name of New Document** textbox, Click **change** in the **full path** section to change the new document location, and choose whether you want to edit the document now or later in the **When to edit** section.

- Select **Email Address** to link the text to send an email to a recipient. Enter the email address or choose from the recently used address.

5. Enter **Ok** to apply, and the text now appears as a link.

To follow a link in MS word.

- Click and hold the **Ctrl** button.

- Click on the link, and it will take you to its destination.

You can edit the link by right-clinking on it and choosing from the menu that appears, based on what you want to do.

Word formats hyperlinked text differently from all other texts by default, and you can change the setting in the **Word Options.**

PAGE BREAKS AND SECTION BREAKS

When working on a document with multiple pages and many headings, it is sometimes challenging to format the document so that all chapter headings start on a new page without some beginning at the bottom. Also, when working on some types of documents with multiple sections like an article, report, paper, or book, it might be difficult to add **different** headers, footers, footnotes, page numbers, and other formatting elements.

Word duplicates the same headers, footers, and footnotes and continues numbering throughout the document. To have a separate one, document **breaks** are required.

There are two types of document breaks in Word:

- Page breaks

- Section breaks.

Page breaks partition the document's body, while section breaks partition not only the document body but also the headings (or chapters), headers, footnotes, page numbers, margins, etc.

Page Breaks are subdivided into:

- **Page break**: This forces all the text behind the insertion point to the next page.

- **Column** break: This forces the text to the right of the insertion point to the next column of the same page when working with a document with multiple columns

- **Text Wrapping break**: It moves any text to the right of the cursor to the following line and is instrumental when working with objects.

Sections are the part of Word that controls pages, headers, footers, orientation, margins, and columns on Microsoft Word. Section breaks allow you to space up your document into independent chunks. In addition, it shows which document parts have different page orientations, columns, or Headers and footers.

Uses of Section Breaks

- If your document needs different headers and footers on different pages, you will use Section breaks to do this.

- Using Section breaks, you can make a table of contents, index, and Appendices with different types of numerals.

- You'll need a section break between two pages for a document with two pages.

- If you need to mix pages that are portrait-oriented with landscape-oriented pages, you can use section breaks

- Section breaks can be added before and after Word's newspaper column feature so you can use them in the middle of a page.

- You can start page numbers again at any point in a document by putting a section break in the middle of a document.

Section Breaks are subdivided into:

- **Next Page break:** This divides the documents by creating another page that can have its special formatting. This is useful for partitioning your document into different chapters with different headers, footers, page numbers, etc.

- **Continuous break:** This divides the document into sections that can be independently formatted on the same page without creating a new page. This break is usually used to change the number of columns on a page.

- **Even Page break:** This shifts the insertion point and any text at its right to the next even page.

- **Odd Page breaks** This shifts the insertion point and any text at its right to the next odd page.

To Insert a Page Break or Section Break:

1. Place your insertion point to where you want the break.

2. Go to the **Layout** ribbon.

3. Select **Breaks** in the **Page Setup** group.

A drop-down list appears with all the types of breaks.

4. Select from the options the type of section break you want.

Figure 69: Section breaks

Insert a continuous section break

This is the same as above, but the section break stays on the same page; you use it if you want to do something like changing a two-column layout before going back to the normal layout.

Insert a column break

If you have a layout that uses columns and wants to force the text to move to the new column, use a column break (also in the Breaks menu).

- It can also be achieved using Ctrl + Shift + Enter.

Delete breaks

- With the non-printable symbols displayed, click in front of the jump.

- Press Delete on your keyboard.

9.4 The Proofing Tools

Microsoft Word is smart. It helps you find mistakes. These helpers are called "Proofing Tools". The proofing tools allow you to use the spelling and grammar checking features in Word for a wide range of languages to check for spelling errors and grammatical error

The proofing tool is in the **Review tab**, on the left-hand side under the **Proofing** category

Figure 70: Proofing category

Spelling Checker

We all make spelling mistakes. But Word can find them for us. A red squiggly line appears under the wrong word. Right-click on it. Word will give suggestions. Pick the right one. Your mistake is fixed!

Grammar Checker

Grammar is tricky. But Word has a tool for that too. If a sentence sounds weird, Word will tell you. A blue squiggly line will show up. Right-click on it. Word will tell you what's wrong. It will also give a fix. It's like having a teacher inside your computer.

Thesaurus

Sometimes, we use the same word too much. Word has a thesaurus. It gives you other words that mean the same thing. Highlight the word. Right-click. Choose "Synonyms". A list will pop up. Pick a new word. Your writing just got better!

Word Count

How long is your document? Word can tell you. Go to the "Review" tab. Click "Word Count". A box will show up. It tells you how many words, characters, and paragraphs you have. It's super useful, especially for school assignments.

Read Aloud

Hearing your work is different from reading it. Word can read your document out loud. Go to the "Review" tab. Click "Read Aloud". Sit back and listen. It's like having a story read to you.

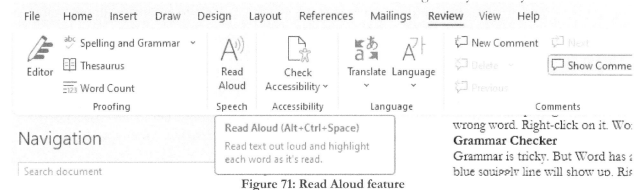

Figure 71: Read Aloud feature

Language

Writing in Spanish? French? No problem! Word can check spelling in other languages. Highlight the text. Go to the "Review" tab. Click "Language". Choose the right one. Word will check it for you.

AutoCorrect

We type fast. Sometimes, we type the same mistakes. Word can fix them automatically. It's called AutoCorrect. For example, if you type "teh", Word changes it to "the". It's like magic!

Custom Dictionary

Some words are special. Maybe it's a name or a brand. Word might think it's a mistake. But you can teach Word. Add the word to the "Custom Dictionary". Now, Word knows it's right.

Researcher

Need to know more about a topic? Word can help. Highlight the word. Right-click. Choose "Researcher". Word will show you information. It's like a mini-library.

Translator

Need to translate a word? Word can do that. Highlight the word. Right-click. Choose "Translate". Pick a language. Word will show you the translation. It's like having a translator with you.

10 USE OF STYLES

The user creates styles highlighting a document's structure, tone, and format. The styles that come with Word are named after the types of documents they apply to. For example, there is the Title style, which is set to bold formatting, or the Normal style, which causes no formatting. In addition, you can create your styles for documents by choosing 'New Style' from the Format menu.

A style is a collection of formatting commands under a single name. When a style is applied, lots of formatting commands are simultaneously given, and you will save yourself the stress of going to different tabs and dialog boxes to begin to format text. Styles help to save time, and they also make documents look more professional. Headings with the same style, for example -**Heading1,** all have the same look. When readers notice a form of consistency in headings and paragraphing, they will have a warm and cozy feeling about the document. They will think that whoever must have created the document knows what they are doing. Style is a set of formatting features such as font size, color, and alignment that can be applied to text, tables, and lists to quickly change the document's appearance. Applying styles to your document helps to give it a professional look.

Why Should You Use Styles?

The following are the reasons why you need to use Styles while creating documents

- Styles give your document uniform headings and subheadings

- Styles allow for efficient formatting while working with your document.

- Applying a style in your document gives you a quick way to see the headings and subheadings on the Navigation Pane.

- Applying styles to your document gives you an easy shortcut to automatically get a table of contents and a list of tables and figures.

Components of Styles

The following are the components of Styles

- **Paragraph styles**: These paragraph styles control the formatting of a complete paragraph. The paragraph style has the following settings; font, paragraph, tab, indentation, line spacing, justification, border, language, bullet, numbering, and text effects. The paragraph style is denoted with the paragraph symbol (¶)

Figure 72: Paragraph styles

- **Character styles:** The character style can only be applied to text in a document. To apply this style, you will first have to select the text. The character style has the following settings: font name, font size, italics, bold, color, border, language, and text effect.

- **Linked (Paragraph and character)**: These style types can be applied to paragraphs and text within a document. These styles can be denoted with paragraph symbol (¶) and the letter a. Note: The Linked style must be enabled.

- **Table styles:** These control the formatting outlook of a table in a document. The table styles have the following settings borders, shadings, alignment, and fonts.

- **List styles**: These control the formatting of the list by applying similar alignment, numbering, bullet characters, and fonts.

How to See All Styles In Microsoft Word

On the Home tab, look at the style option and click on one style; for example, it will highlight all text around the style.

Microsoft word doesn't load all the styles; all you have to do is click on the small icon on the bottom right corner of the style panel (Circled in the figure below), and all the style shows up. You can further click on the options button, and you see the option select style to show. Click on all styles and click on OK. Then all styles that are missing will show up

Figure 73: Style pane arrow

Why Uses Styles in Words

     i. You can be sure that all the headings, paragraphs, subheadings, etc. have the same correct, consistent formatting.

    ii. It is faster to apply style than doing it individually.

Applying Styles to your Text or Paragraphs

You can apply styles to your text or paragraph by following the steps below.

- Select the text or paragraph you wish to format (You can position your cursor at the beginning of the paragraph)

We use this paragraph for showcasing the application of styles to the text. It will provide the different aspects where all the headings, paragraphs, subheadings, etc. have the same correct, consistent formatting

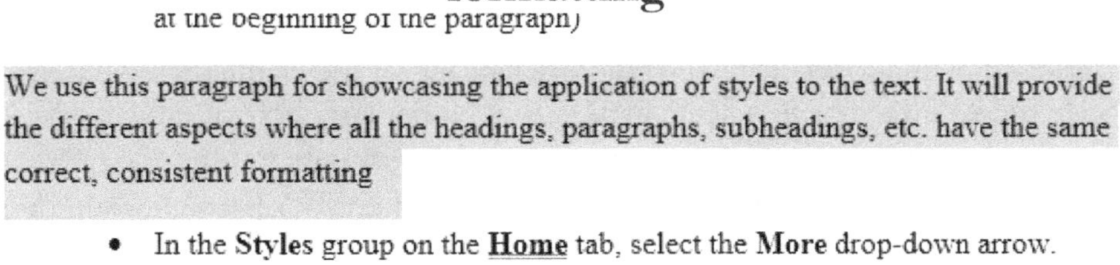

at the beginning of the paragraph)

We use this paragraph for showcasing the application of styles to the text. It will provide the different aspects where all the headings, paragraphs, subheadings, etc. have the same correct, consistent formatting

- In the **Styles** group on the <u>**Home**</u> tab, select the **More** drop-down arrow.

Figure 74: Highlighted paragraph

- In the **Styles** group on the **Home** tab, select the **More** drop-down arrow.

Figure 75: More drop-down on styles

- Choose your best style from the drop-down menu. You can choose **Para 53**.

Figure 76: More styles

- The text selected will appear in the desired style selected.

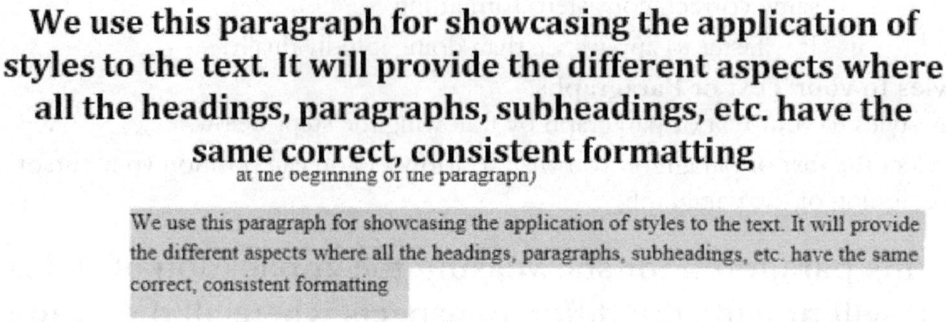

We use this paragraph for showcasing the application of styles to the text. It will provide the different aspects where all the headings, paragraphs, subheadings, etc. have the same correct, consistent formatting
at the beginning of the paragraph)

We use this paragraph for showcasing the application of styles to the text. It will provide the different aspects where all the headings, paragraphs, subheadings, etc. have the same correct, consistent formatting

Figure 77: Applying styles

Applying a Style Set

Style sets are made up of a title, headings, and paragraph styles. Style sets permit you to format all the elements in your document at once instead of modifying each of the elements separately. Before applying the Style set, you must have assigned styles to your paragraph, text, table, or list. Follow the procedures below to apply the style set to your text or paragraph

- Click on the More drop-down arrow in the Document Formatting group on the Design tab.

Figure 78: Document Formatting

- Choose the best style from the drop-down menu.

Figure 79: Document Formatting styles to choose

- The style set selected will appear on the entire document.

Creating a New Style
There are two ways to create a new style in your document: by creating it from the paragraph or from the ground up. So now, let's create a new style using the earlier two methods.

Creating a New Style from a Paragraph
To create a new style from a paragraph, follow the steps given below

- Select the paragraph you wish to change its formatting into a style

- From the **Home** tab**,** open the **Styles** gallery and click on **Creating a Style**

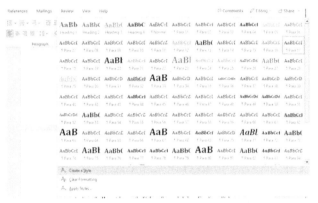

Figure 80: Creating a new paragraph style

- In the **Create New Style from the Formatting** dialog box, enter the name of the new style and then click on **Ok**

Figure 81: Create a new style from formatting

Creating a Style from the Ground up
To create a new style from the ground up, follow the steps given below

- From the **Home** tab and click on the **Styles** group button

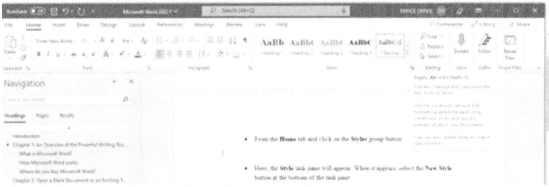

Figure 82: Styles from Home button

- Here, the **Style** task pane will appear. When it appears, select the **New Style** button at the bottom of the task pane.

Figure 83: Create New Style from the Formatting

- In the **Create New Style from the Formatting** dialog box, set the following options

- **Name:** Input the description name of the new style.

- **Style Type:** This allows you to choose any type of style (Paragraph, character, line, table, and list)

- **Style Based On:** This allows you to choose the style to get a head start if the new style is related to a style already found in the template.

- **The style for Formatting Paragraph:** This allows you to select a style from the drop-down list if the style you are creating is related to or followed by an existing style.

- **Formatting:** This allows you to choose an option from the menu to refine your style.

- **Add to Style Gallery:** This check box allows the style's name to appear in the Styles gallery, Style pane, and Apply Styles task pane.

- **Automatically Update:** This updates the changes made to the styles in the document.

- **Only in This Document/New Documents Based on This Template:** This allows you to make your style part of the template from which you created your document and the document itself.

- **Format:** Clicking on this button directs you to a dialog box where you can create or refine the style.

Figure 84: Creating your new style

- Then click on Ok

Modifying a Style

To modify a style, follow the steps below:

- Go to the **Home** tab, right-click on the Style you wish to change in the **Style**s group, and then click on **Modify** in the drop-down menu

Figure 85: Modifying style

- Adjust the settings in the Modify dialog box and click on **OK**

Figure 86: Adjust style settings

Renaming Your Styles

To change the name of your styles, follow the steps below

- Go to the **Home** tab, right-click on the Style you wish to change in the **Style**s group, and then click on **Rename** in the drop-down menu

Figure 87: Renaming styles

- In the **Rename Style** dialog box, enter the name and click on **Ok**

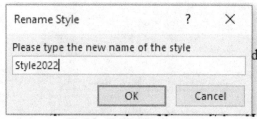

Figure 88: Rename style

To use a style in Microsoft for Headings: Highlight all the different headings on your document. There is a section called styles on the home tab, as shown below. Click on the style you want, and that style will be applied to the selected headings.

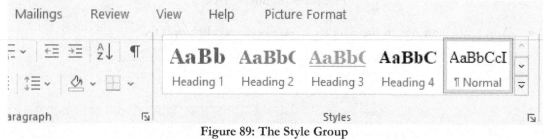

Figure 89: The Style Group

Note: One great benefit of styles is that it applies to all selected headings as you make changes to a style.

How to Delete Styles

Click on the arrow on the home tab on the style groups. Next, click on the particular style, and in the drop-down arrow, click delete. If it asks if you're sure you want to delete it, click yes. Once done, the style will no longer appear on the style menu.

Alternatively, on the style pane on the home tab, click on the managed file at the bottom of the style pane. Select the name of the style to delete and then delete. Click the yes button on the Confirmation box that appears. However, to permanently remove the style from the template, you must take an extra step. Click on the import and export button at the bottom of the dialogue box, and on the left side, you will see a template of a document name list in the styles available in the drop-down. Choose the template name within which the style you want to delete has been saved from the styles available on the drop-down. Then in the template document name list, select the customized style to delete. On the Confirmation box that appears, click yes to the question and close.

Restricting Styles Changes on Microsoft Word

To turn on style restrictions:

- Click on the **File** Tab and then select protect a document in the back icon as shown in figure 92

- On the drop-down menu, select **Restrict Editing (**Figure 92)

- Next, on the restrict editing pane, select formatting restrictions and then select the settings

- On the formatting restrictions dialogue box, check/mark "limit formatting to a selection of styles," as shown in figure 93

- Now check or uncheck the individual styles you want to allow in the document, select one of the preset option buttons or click "All" to check every style currently allowed in the document. Click on "Recommended Minimum" this option checks comment style options currently allowed in the document but unchecks fewer comments styles such as a table. "None" unchecked all style options (figure 93)

- Then check or uncheck the three optional formatting choices (i. allow other formats to override formatting restrictions; this first option implies that you should allow other formats to surpass the option selected in the formatting restrictions style or box ii. Block theme or scheme switching prevents other users from changing the document to a different theme in the design tab or a separate scheme such as the color scheme iii. And the last option is to block Quick Style set switching, which, when clicked on, helps prevent other users from using the style options on the home tab) When you're done, select Ok. This is circled red in figure 93

- A dialogue box will ask, "The Document may contain formatting or styles that aren't allowed. Do you want to remove them"? Select No if you want to keep all of your existing styles while preventing other users from using them

- Next, select yes on the start enforcement button and enter a password on the start enforcing protection dialogue box and then select OK, as shown in figure 95

Figure 90: Protect Document Button

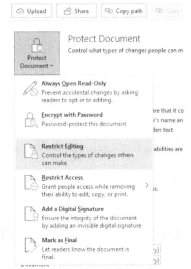

Figure 91: Restrict Editing Button

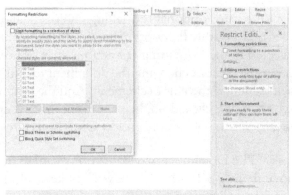

Figure 92: Formatting Restrictions Icon

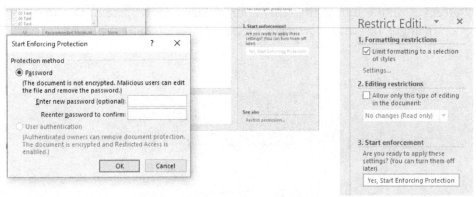

Figure 93: Start enforcement button

Turning Off These Style Restrictions

Return to the restrict editing task pane, and select the stop protection button (figure 96). Enter your password in the unprotected document dialogue box and click OK. When this is done, it turns off the style restrictions from the password-protected copy of the file you shared with other users.

Figure 94: Stop protection button

Note: You will have to share your password with them if you would like them to turn off the protection also.

11 NUMERATIONS AND BULLETINS

Numeration: This refers to the numbering of a document. Word display counters for numbering, such as 1.1.2, but creating specific symbols and numbers in separate places makes it easy for users to reference. Word uses numbers in basic format: the first digit followed by a decimal point and then a second digit or number with a letter or symbol signifying the position (1, 2, 3, etc. . .). Bullets: This function allows users to create the 'bullets' or the numbered items in a document. Word uses bullets in different styles, but all can be customized according to the user's preference. A bullet point is a short line that serves as proof or an idea that is easy for readers to comprehend and digest.

Bullets and numbers are used to list things in the document. For example, they are used to attract the reader's attention to the pace to which something is moving or the importance attached to a specific through the arrangement of the list. Bullet and number lists are located under the paragraph section in the Home tab.

CREATING A BULLET LIST

The bullet is an icon people use to list an item in a document. The bullet can be a dot, a small square, a marked sign, and so on. When you arrange a list with a bullet, such an item will be indented. To make a list with a bullet, study the steps below:

- Place your cursor pointer to the line where you want to start the bullet list.

- Tap on the **Home tab** and move to the paragraph section.

Figure 95: Home bullet option

- Then click on the **bullets down button** and select **any bullet style** you want. The bullet you selected will be reflected.

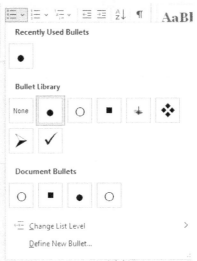

Figure 96: Bullet types

- Type whatever you want, and press **Enter** to move to the next line with an automatic bullet list. The more Enter you click, the more bullet list you will have.

Note: bullet has its paragraph and indent formatting. Click on the bullet icon again to stop the automatic bullet listing.

To customize your list bullet:

Select **Define New Bullet**

A Define New Bullet dialog box appears.

Set the **character** and **alignment** as desired, then press **OK**

- Select **Symbol** to use a symbol as your listing icon. A symbol dialog box appears. Choose your desired symbol, press OK, and your symbol will be set as your listing icon.

- Select **Picture** to use an online picture or any picture on your computer as a list icon.

- Select **Font** to set the **font style**, **size,** and the **effects** of your list icons.

CREATING A NUMBER LIST

A numbering list is a common type of listing an item of a document. To number a list, do well:

1. Place your cursor pointer to the line where you want to start the number list.

2. Tap on the **Home tab** and move to the paragraph section.

3. Then click on **numbering** and select any **numbering style** you want. The number style you selected will be reflected on the first line.

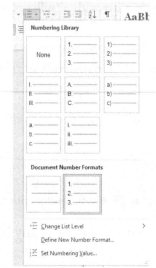

Figure 97: Numbering styles

4. Press **Enter** to move to the next item with automatic numbering; the more Enter you click the number list, the more number list you will have.

Note: click on no number to remove the number list, and click on the "number list" icon to stop automatic numbering.

To customize your numbered list:
  Select **Define New Number Format**
A **Define New Number Format** dialog box appears.
  Select and set the **forma**t /**alignment** as desired.
Selecting bullets or the numbering command will change the list style if your cursor is already in numbered or bulleted lists.

Also available is a **Multilevel list** command for you to use if your list has a sub-list.

Figure 98: Multilevel list

You can format the listing style by right-clicking on the list and selecting an option as desired.

ADDING MULTILEVEL LIST

As its name denotes multilevel, the listing is of various types. It has the main listing, sub, and sub-sub listing. Word will automatically carry out the multilevel listing for you. To do multilevel listing, study the below guideline:

1. Insert the **first item in the list** to the line without numbering it.

2. Tap on the **Home tab**, move to the paragraph section, and then click on the **multilevel menu button.**

3. Choose the **desired multilevel style**, and immediately the first number will be attached with a number or alphabet depending on the multilevel style you choose.

Figure 99: desired multilevel style

4. Press the **tab key** for the sub-listing item and **Enter another tab key** for the sub-sub listing.

Note: you will use a tab to move from main to sub and sub-sub listing. You will use **Tab +Shift** to move back from the sub-listing and main listing.

12 THE POWER OF FIND AND REPLACE

We started looking at some of the basic ways to use your keyboard to navigate around your document in the previous chapters. In this chapter, you'll be introduced to a few more utilities you can use in Word to navigate your document and increase your efficiency when working with your documents. In addition, this chapter will concentrate on the Go to, Find, and Replace options.

Looking for a Word

When working with enormous files, you may require a quick way to get to a specific page or to replace a word in a document.

To access your "**Find**" and "**Replace**" options, click at the top of your document, then go to the **home** ribbon. Across on the right-hand side is an editing group, where you'll find them. In addition, you can see that "**Find**" has a little drop-down arrow next to it, indicating that it offers three options: **Find, Advanced Find**, and "**Go to.**"

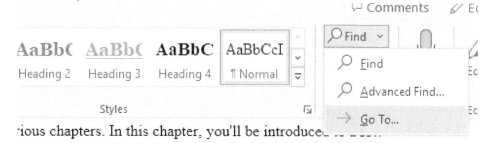

Figure 100: Go To

In this example, we'll start on "**Find**," which opens up a little navigation window on the left-hand side where you can put in exactly what you're looking for. It brings up results once you type in the term you're looking for, and you can see them listed underneath in the results section and highlighted in your document, making it incredibly easy to find them. By clicking on the cross, you can close this navigation panel. That's one approach to searching your document for a specific word.

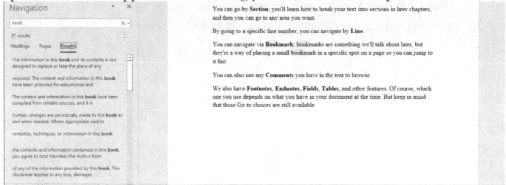

Figure 101: Find results

Using advanced Find to Search Your Document

If you select Advanced Find, you'll be sent to a little dialog box that asks you what you're looking for and displays the last item you looked for. If you want to skip this one by one, you can say **"Find Next,"** which will highlight the word in the document the first time it finds it. You can then say **"Find Next"** again to step through each one in your document one at a time, and when you get to the end, it will tell you it's finished searching, and you can click OK.

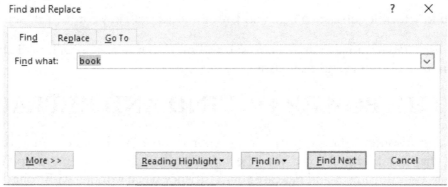

Figure 102: Find Next

Getting specify With Find

The **"More"** option in this Find and Replace box is also something to be mindful of. When you click it, you'll see that you have many options. For example, you can tell it to **match the case**, meaning it will only find the word "firm" if it matches that case. So if the word "firm" is in this document with an uppercase F, it won't find it because you told it to match the case.

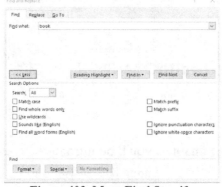

Figure 103: More Find Specify

You can choose to **"Find whole words only**," which means that if what you're looking for is a part of another word, it won't be found. You can also say **"Use Wildcards"** and place a wildcard in front of the word, midway in the middle, or at the end. If you type in A*, for example, it will discover everything in that document that begins with an A, regardless of what comes after it. You can also include a wildcard at the start, such as *S, which implies it will look for anything that ends in S, regardless of what follows before it. It's worth noting that wildcards come in handy when looking for specific items. Another thing you can do up here is to type "A" and then two question marks (A??) to indicate that the word must begin with an A and contain no more than three characters in total. It doesn't matter what those three characters are, but they must be three.

You can also use the **"Sounds Like"** option to find words that sound similar to the one you're looking for. It might pick up words like turn, burn, study, or anything along those lines for a word like "firm," for example.

"Find all word forms" will find any form of that word, and you can then choose between **"Match prefix,"** **"Match suffix,"** **"Ignore punctuation,"** and "Ignore whitespace characters," among other possibilities. Finally, remember that beneath the "More" drop-down, you have various options for customizing what you're looking for in your document, which can become very detailed.

Replace One Word with Another

Make sure you're at the top of my document and select the **"Replace"** option this time. We have **"Replace"** under **"Find"** in the editing group, which allows you to **replace one word with another**. For instance, if you want to replace the name "Smith" in your document with "Ashby," you may say find "Smith" and replace it with "Ashby," and you'll have all of the prior possibilities to choose from. If you merely want to replace Smith with Ashby, pick **"Replace all."** You'll get a little window telling you that the replacements have been made, and if you look at the document behind you, Smith has been replaced. This is a quick and easy technique to replace several words in a document.

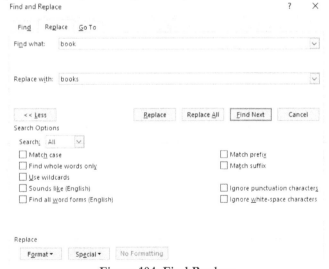

Figure 104: Find Replace

Go to any point in your document

The **"Go to"** option, which lets you perform different things in your document, is the last item you should know in this chapter. When you go to Find and select the **"Go To"** option, you'll be able to browse around your document. You can accomplish this by entering a page number and saying **"Go To"**; for example, if you input page 2 and say "Go To," it will take you to page 2.

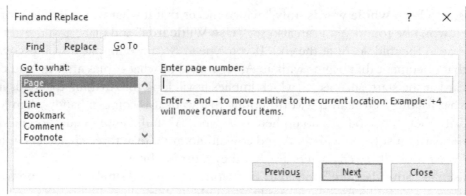

Figure 105: Go To Point

You can go by **Section**; you'll learn how to break your text into sections in later chapters, and then you can go to any area you want.

By going to a specific line number, you can navigate by **Line**.

You can navigate via **Bookmark**; bookmarks are something we'll talk about later, but they're a way of placing a small bookmark in a specific spot on a page so you can jump to it fast.

You can also use any **Comments** you have in the text to browse.

We also have **Footnotes**, **Endnotes**, **Fields**, **Tables**, and other features. Of course, which one you use depends on what you have in your document at the time. But keep in mind that those Go to choices are still available.

13 FOOTER AND HEADER OF THE PAGE

Page footers:

This refers to the text that appears at the bottom of every page of your document. It includes the page number, time and date, or any other information you need. In addition, word allows you to create a custom page footer for any document. Go to the Layout tab - Page Setup and select your custom page footer under the 'Footer' option.

Header: This refers to title information usually found at the top of every page in a document. This includes the page name, title, and author name. Word allows you to set your header information with a particular font style, size, alignment, and other settings.

INSERTING HEADER OR FOOTER

A **Header** is a text added to the top margin of every page of a document. At the same time, a **footer** is a text added to the bottom Margin to give information about the document, e.g., the title, page number, image, logo, etc.

To add a Header or Footer to your document:

1. Go to the **Insert** ribbon.

2. Select **Header** or **Footer** command.

A drop-down menu appears with header or footer styles.

3. Click on the desired style.

Word activates the top and bottom margin for your header or footer insertion.

4. Replace the text with your desired text.

5. Click on the **Close Header and Footer** command when you are done.

Alternatively,

1. Double-click in the top or bottom margin to activate the header and footer area.

2. Insert your footer or header.

3. Double-click outside the margin area or press the **Esc** key to go back to your document.

You can always use the above method to edit your header or footer. Also available is a contextual **Design** tab you can use to design your header or footer.

To delete your header or footer, just delete the text and close the header and footer.

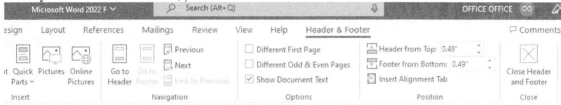

Figure 106: Close Header and Footer

Inserting Different Headers or Footers in Word

To insert a separate Header or Footer for a Separate Section:

1. Insert **Next Page** section breaks where you want different headers or footers to start.
2. Activate the headers or footers of each section.

In the **Navigation** group of the **Header & Footer** Tools ribbon;

3. Deselect the **Link to** the **Previous** button to disconnect the sections.
4. Add the header or footer for each section or chapter.
5. To put a different header on the document's first page or a section, Check the **Different First Page** box.
6. To put a right-justified header for some pages and a left-justified header for some pages, check the **Different Odd & Even Pages** box.

Figure 107: Link to the Previous

7. Close the header/footer when done with the settings.

Saving Headers or Footers for Later Use

In case you are using a particular header or footer to create so many documents, it will be advisable to save the header/footer.

To save your header or footer for later use:

1. Activate and select all the header or footer contents you want to save.
2. Click the **Header** or **Footer** drop-down button as the case may be.
3. Select Save Selection to Header Gallery or Save Selection to Footer Gallery, depending on whether you select Header or Footer.

Figure 108: Save Selection to Header Gallery

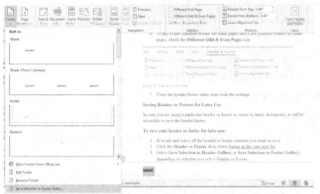

Figure 109: Save Selection to Footer Gallery

A dialog box appears.

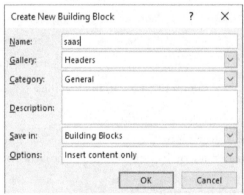

Figure 110: Saving Header Gallery Dialog box

4. Input the name you want to give the header or footer and do any other desired settings.
5. Press **OK,** and your header or footer will be saved.

You can access and apply the header or footer at any time in the drop-down list of the **Header** or **Footer** drop button. You might have to scroll down to see your preferred options.

To delete your saved header or footer:

1. Right-click on it.
2. Select Organize and Delete.

A dialog box appears highlighting the header or footer.

1. Click the **Delete** button.
2. Press **yes** to confirm the prompt that appears.
3. Press **Close** in the dialog box and your header or footer will no longer be in the gallery.

14 IMAGES AND TABLES

Images and tables: how to insert them, how to add new lines and columns in an existing table, what's a caption and what are the caption types, how to insert a caption, what's the automatic updating of the number inside a caption, how to take a screenshot, what's copyright and how to choose image copyright free/public domain/royalty free, etc.

While working on your document, there are times you need to illustrate your work with shapes, pictures, or images and a movable textbox. Word provides features that enable you to do that without stress. Below are step-by-step guides on how to work with illustrations in your document.

14.1 Inserting and Editing Images

To add an image to your document:
1. Place your cursor where you want your picture to be.
2. Go to the **Insert** ribbon.
3. Click the **Picture** command in the **Illustration** group.

The **Insert Picture From** menu box appears.
4. a. Select **This Device** if your image is on your computer.

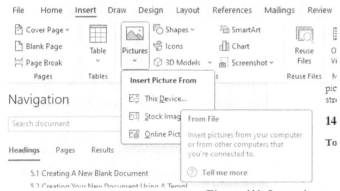

Figure 111: Insert image from this device

An **Insert Picture** dialog box appears.

b. Select **Online Picture** if you want to use an online image.

Your default browser opens.
5. a. Select and open the image folder. Frow the left menu, you can open another location to search for the image. Select your image.

b. Browse for your desired image.
6. Click the **Insert** button or double-click on the image.

Alternatively, copy the image wherever it is and paste it into your document.

INSERTING SCREENSHOTS

You can insert screenshots of any opened window on your system in your document.

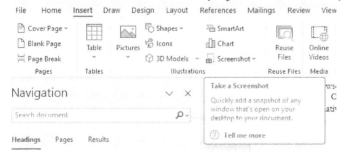

Figure 112: Inserting screenshots

To capture and insert a screenshot in your document:
1. Place your mouse where you want your screenshot to be.
2. Open and display the image or document you want to capture on your computer screen.
3. Click on the **Insert** tab.
4. Select **Screenshot** in the **Illustration** group.

A drop-down menu appears, showing you the available whole window screenshots.
5. a. Select the desired available screenshot if you want to capture the whole screen, and Word automatically inserts the screenshot in your document.

b. Select **Screen Clipping** to capture a part of any of the windows.

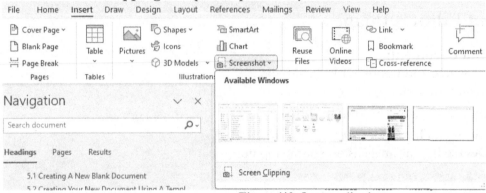

Figure 113: Screen clipping

Your cursor turns to a plus icon, and your screen turns blurred.
6. Click, hold, and drag the mouse to select your desired portion of the window.
7. Release your hand when done, and Word automatically inserts your selected window portion into your document.

NOTE: To insert your desktop screenshot, close or minimize all documents that can interfere with the screen. You do not need to close the document you are working with, for Word closes it automatically when you select **Screen Clipping** as you follow the above steps.

INSERTING SHAPES
Different shapes, like circles, rectangles, lines, arrows, and more, are available in Word for your use.
To add shapes to your document:
1. Click the **Insert** tab.
2. Select the **Shapes** to command in the **Illustrations** group.

The Shapes dialog box appears with all the available shapes.
3. Click on any of the shapes as desired.

Your cursor turns to a cross.
4. Move to the location in your document where you want your shape to be.
5. Click and drag to draw the shape to the desired size.

Tips: The shape turns itself off after each use to keep it active for continuous use,
- Select and right-click on it
- Select **Lock Drawing Mode** from the menu that appears.
- Draw the shape as many times as desired.
- Press the **Esc** key or click on the shape icon again when you are done.

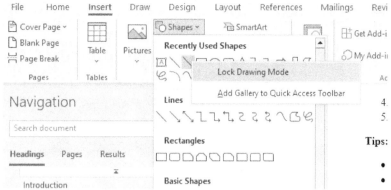

Figure 114: Lock Drawing Mode

You can as well add text to your shape.

To add text to your shape:

1. Click inside the shape.
2. Type in your text.

Format your text just like any other text in your document as desired.

ADDING SMARTART TO YOUR DOCUMENT.

SmartArt visually communicates essential ideas, information, and processes with a graphical presentation.

Word has a SmartArt gallery consisting of a list, process, cycle, hierarchy, etc., to meet your specific requirement.

To add a SmartArt to your document:

1. Place the insertion point where you want your SmartArt.
2. Go to **Insert** ribbon.
3. Click on **SmartArt** in the **Illustration** group.

A dialog box appears.

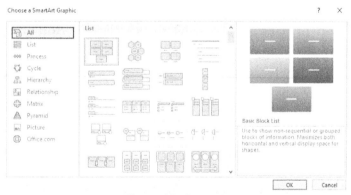

Figure 115: SmartArt

4. Click on the SmartArt type that best describes what you want to do, e.g., list, process, cycle, etc.
5. Select one of the SmartArt type varieties as desired.
6. Press **OK,** and Word inserts the SmartArt with a pane.
7. Replace the **SmartArt** pane text with your texts.

For more items, press **Enter** in the last item, and Word automatically creates more places for you to continue.

With the SmartArt is contextual **Design** and **Format** tabs for you to format your **SmartArt.**

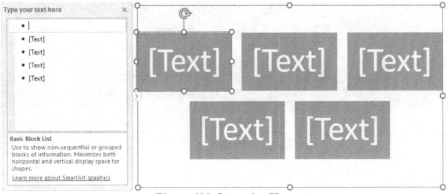

Figure 116: SmartArt Text

Designing SmartArt

Various options are available to set up, organize and design your SmartArt to your taste after inserting it.

To design your SmartArt:

1. Select the SmartArt.
2. Go to the contextual **SmartArt Design** tab.
3. Make the desired changes:

   - Click on **Change Color** or the **SmartArt Styles** gallery drop-down arrow to see the list of different color templates you can select and apply to your SmartArt.

   - To rearrange your points in the SmartArt, select the shape and click the **Move Up** or **Move Down** commands in the **Create Graphic** group.

   - To change the list level of a selected shape or bullet, click the **Promote**, or **Demote** command in the **Create Graphic** group.

   - You can change the SmartArt layout from left to right and vice visa by selecting or deselecting the **Right to Left** command.

   - If you need more than the three available shapes, click the **Add Shape** button in the **Create Graphic** group to add more shapes.

   - If you need more than the available bullet on the shape, click the **Add Bullet** button in the **Create Graphic** group to add more bullets.

   - You can hide or Unhide the text pane on your slide by clicking the **Text Pane** button in the **Create Graphic** group.

   - You can convert your SmartArt to text or shapes by clicking the **Convert** drop-down arrow and selecting the desired option.

   - If your SmartArt has picture icons, click on the icon, and follow the prompt to add your desired picture.

   - Click the **Reset Graphic** button to undo all the settings if you wish to.

Figure 117: SmartArt Design

WORKING WITH TEXTBOX

A textbox is an object that allows you to type your text and place it anywhere in your document. Using a textbox makes working with text flexible.

To insert a textbox:

1. Click the **Insert** tab.

2. Select the **Text box** in the **Text** group.

A dialog box appears with preformatted textbox options.

3. Select an option as desired, and the textbox appears in your document or

-Select **More Text Box from Office.com** to get more text box options on the Microsoft Office website.

Select **Draw Text Box** if you want to draw your text box to your desired size manually. Your cursor turns to a cross.

- Click the point you want to put your textbox and drag it to draw to your desired size.

4. Type in your text and click anywhere outside the box when you are done.

To Edit your text box:

1. Double click on the text box and edit like a normal word document.
2. Use your arrow keys to navigate in the textbox.

WORKING WITH WORDART

A WordArt is a form of a textbox with additional styles. Word has a gallery of WordArt with different styles that you can quickly apply to your texts to change their appearance and styles.

To use WordArt in your document:

1. Click on the **Insert** tab.
2. Select **WordArt** in the **Text** group.

WordArt drop-down menu appears.

3. Click on the desired style, which appeared in your document as a text box with the text format as the style of letter **A** in the gallery.
4. Type in your text and click anywhere outside the box when you are done.

To Edit your text box:

1. Double click on the text box and edit like a normal word document.
2. Use your arrow keys to navigate in the textbox.

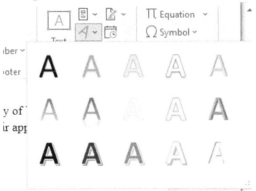

Figure 118: WordArt

OBJECT LAYOUT (MAKE OBJECT FLOATS WITH TEXT WRAPPING)

Word inserts an object **in line** with text by default, but options can change the object layout relative to the text. Using any of the **With Text Wrapping** options makes your object float, i.e., you can select and move it freely to any location, whether there is text or no text in the place. It also allows you to write on your image.

To make your object float:

1. Select the object.

2. Click the **Layout Options** icon that appears at the top right side of the object, or Go to the contextual **Format** ribbon and select **Wrap Text.**

A drop-down menu appears.

3. Select an option in the **With Text Wrapping** option depending on how you want your image to relate to the text.

Figure 119: Object Layout

Hover on each option to see their names and how the layout works with the text with the icon. For example, this icon [image] called **Behind Text** shows that the object will be at the back of the text if it is moved to where there is text.

There are also two options for moving the object with text or fixing the object's position on the page. Check any of the desired options.

For more layout, select **See more**.

FORMATTING AND EDITING OBJECTS

Objects are shape, picture, image, screenshot, WordArt, Textbox, and SmartArt. When selected, any objects will have a contextual object **Format** tab that can be used to format the object. Most of the Format commands are the same across all the objects, and most are for visual effects enhancement of the object.

Selecting an Object

To format an object, the first thing you do is select the object. Follow the steps below to select an object:

- Click inside of the object.
- Move your cursor to any part of the object outline. Your cursor turns to four-headed arrows.
- Click on the outline.

Deleting an Object

1. Select the image you want to delete.

Selection handles appear around the image.

2. Press Delete or Backspace button on your keyboard, and your image is removed.

Applying Visual Effects Enhancement to an Object

MS Word has impressive features that you can use to make changes to your object after you have inserted it into your document. You can make the following changes with Word features.

For pictures and some other objects:

• **Corrections:** It adjusts your image brightness, contrast, sharpness, or softness in different proportions.

• **Color:** It changes the color of your image with different shades from color to black and white.

• **Artistic Effects:** It changes your image to look like a sketch or paint of different styles.

• **Compress Pictures:** It reduces the size of your image.

• **Change Picture:** It makes you change your picture to another one retaining the size and format of your current picture.

• **Reset Picture:** To undo all the changes you have made to the image.

• **Picture Border:** It helps to put an outline around the image, and the outline color, width, and style can be changed as desired.

- **Picture Effects:** It applies effects like shadow, reflection, glows, etc., to your image.
- **Picture Layout:** It makes your image easy to edit by converting it to a SmartArt graphic.

Figure 120: Graphic Layout

Other formatting features for most objects include:

- **Object Fill** : Selecting this command fills your shape with the default or last applied color. Click on the drop-down button to select a desired fill color in the color palette.

- **Object Outline** : Selecting this command, put borders around your object with the default or last applied color. Click on the drop-down button to select a desired outline color in the color palette.

- **Object Effect** : This gives your object some artistic effects like shadow, reflection, glow, 3-D rotation, etc. Click on the command, select from the effects option, and choose a desired version of the effects.

- **Object Style:** This contains a gallery of preformatted objects for your quick use.

Figure 121: Shape Formats

To make changes to your object using any of the features above:

1. Select the object.

The object **Format** contextual tab appears.

2. Click the object **Format** tab.

3. Select the effect you want to apply, e.g., **Corrections, Border, Artistic Effects, fill, etc.**

4. If the effect has a drop-down icon, click on it, and select an option as desired.

The object style in the **Format** ribbon depends on the type of object you inserted.

Remove Picture Background with MS Word

Word has a feature that can help you remove the background of your picture for quick use.

To remove an image background:

1. Select the picture or image. Picture Format tab appears.

2. Go to the **Picture Format** tab

Figure 122: Remove image background

3. Select the **Remove Background** command.

Word changes the color of the background it wants to remove and opens the **Background Removal** ribbon for you to adjust.

4.   Click the **Mark Areas to Keep** button, go to your image and mark out some part you would like to keep if there is any.

5.   Click the **Mark Areas to Remove** button, move your cursor to your image and mark out some part you wish to remove but was not highlighted if any.

6.   Select **Keep Changes** to remove the background when you are done or

7.   Select **Discard All Changes** to keep the picture's background.

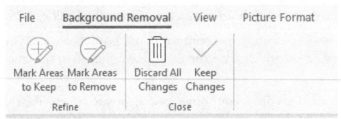

Figure 123: Background removal

Writing on an Image/Picture
To write on an image:
1. Insert your image.
2. Change your image layout to **Behind Text** in the **With Text Wrapping** option.
3. Insert a textbox or WordArt and format as desired.
4. Move your text to the top of the image.
5. Select the Image and the textbox or WordArt.
6. Group them.

Note: Consult other sections of this chapter on how to insert, text wrapping, and group objects.

RESIZING AND CROPPING OBJECT
To resize your image:
1. Select the image you want to resize.

Handle borders appear around the image.
2. Click and drag on any of the handles as desired.

The image changes size as you drag it to the left, right, up, or down.
3. Release your mouse when the size of the image is as desired.

Note: Use the corner handles for uniform increase/decrease in your image size.

Figure 124: Image resizing

Alternatively,

1.   Select the object.

2.   Go to the contextual **Format** tab.

3.   Enter the actual height and width in the text boxes provided (or use the arrows) in the **Size** group.

Figure 125: Image resizing (b)

Cropping

Cropping an image allows you to remove some outer parts of an image.

To crop an image:

1. Click the image you want to crop.
2. Go to the object **Format** tab.
3. Click the **Crop** button in the Size group.

A crop handle appears around the image borders

4. -Drag the **side cropping handle** inside to crop the side

   o Drag the **corner cropping handle** inside to crop two adjacent sides equally and simultaneously.

   o To crop two parallel sides simultaneously, press and hold down the **Ctrl** key as you drag the side cropping handle simultaneously.

5. Press **Esc** on your keyboard when you are done.

Figure 126: Crop element

For more cropping options, click on the **Crop** command drop-down icon and select an option from the menu.

- The **Crop to Shape** allows you to crop your image to the desired shape from the list that appears.

- **Aspect Ratio** gives you some ratio at which you can crop your work.

Figure 127: Aspect Ratio

Can you try something like this?
MOVING, ROTATING, AND FLIPPING IMAGE
To move your image from one place to the other:
        1.   Select the image.

Handle borders appear around the image.
        2.   Click, hold down, and drag the image to the desired location.

To copy, cut, and paste an object
        1.   Click the object to select it.

The object border appears.
        2.   Click the border of the object

-Press **Ctrl + C** to copy or **Ctrl + X** to cut
Alternatively,
  -Right-click on the border. A dialog box appears.
-Select **Cut** or **Copy** as desired.
        3.   Move your cursor where you want the text box to be

        4.   Press **Ctrl + V** to paste the text box.

To rotate your image:
        1.   Click the image you want to rotate.

Handle borders appear around the image.
        2.   Select the rotating handle at the top of the image.

Your cursor turns to a circular arrow.
        3.   Rotate the image clockwise or anticlockwise as desired.

Alternatively, and in other to **flip** the image:
        1.   Select the image you want to rotate/flip.

        2.   Go to the **Picture Format** tab.

        3.   Click the **Rotate** command in the **Arrange** group.

A drop-down menu appears.
        4.   Select an option.

Figure 128: Image rotation

ALIGNING, ORDERING, AND GROUPING OBJECTS IN WORD

Suppose you work with multiple objects like images/pictures, shapes, textbox, and WordArt in your document. In that case, knowing how to align appropriately, order, and group objects is essential. **NOTE:** To align, order, or group objects, you need to select them, and for you to be able to select multiple objects in Word, you must ensure that their layout is any of the **With Text Wrapping** options.

Aligning Objects

To align two or more objects:

1. Hold down the **Ctrl** or **Shift** key and click on the individual objects you want to align to select them.

2. Click on the **object Format** tab

3. Select **Align** command in the **Arrange** group. Align drop-down options appear.

4. Word aligns the objects in their current position by default. For example, select an option in the 3rd group to align with the page or margin.

5. Select one of the alignment options as desired.

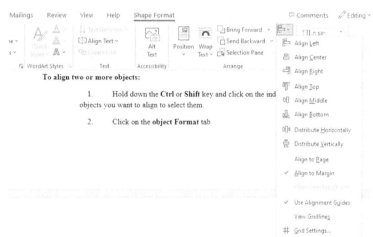

Figure 129: Align object

Note: The alignment options in the 1st and 2nd groups are relative to the 3rd group options. You can use the second group to **equally** distribute your objects horizontally or vertically in the 3rd group.

Ordering Objects

Ordering an object is essential when two or more objects will have to overlap. Objects are placed on top of one another according to the order in which you inserted them into your document, creating different **levels**. Ordering the objects means changing their levels as desired.

To change an object's level:

1. Select the object you want to change its level.
2. Click the **Format** tab.
3. Click the **Send Backward** or **Bring Forward** drop-down in the **Arrange** group. A drop-down menu appears.
4. Select an option, and Word automatically reorders your object.
   - **Send Backward** and **Bring Forward** send your object one level backward and forward, respectively.
   - **Send to Back and Bring to Front; send your object behind and in front of all objects.**

o **Send Behind Text and Bring in Front of Text makes the text and image feasible, respectively.**

Alternatively, to have more control over your ordering,

Select the **Selection Pane** command in the Arrange group.

The selection navigation pane appears on the right side of your window with the list of all the objects starting from the first object at the top to the last at the back.

To rearrange, Select, Drag, and Drop any object to the desired level.

Grouping or Ungrouping Objects

You may sometimes want some of your objects to stay together when working on your document. This can be achieved by grouping.

To group objects:

1. Select your objects by holding the **Ctrl** or **Shift** key and clicking on the individual objects.
2. Click on the **Format** tab.
3. Select **Group** in the **Resize** group.

Then your objects will be a singular object that can be moved, resized, and formatted together like one.

To Ungroup your objects:

1. Select the grouped object.
2. Click on the **Format** tab.
3. Select the **Group** command drop-down icon.
4. Select **Ungroup** from the menu that appears.

14.2 Table Creation and Formatting

A table is a grid of cells organized into rows and columns. Tables are used to organize any form of content, be it text or numerical data, for typing, editing, and formatting appropriately in your document. The following are the components of a table:

- **Cell**: This is the box formed when the row and column intersect.
- **Header row: This is the name of the label along** the top row that describes what is in the column.
- **Row labels**: These are the labels in the first column that explain what is in each row.
- **Borders**: These are the lines indicating where the rows and columns are.
- **Gridlines** are the gray lines that reveal where the columns and rows are. The grid lines do not appear unless they are enabled. To display the gridlines, go to (Table Tools) and click on the View Gridlines button.

Creating a table

We have numerous ways to create a table in Word. Below are the method of creating a table:

- Drag the table menu
- Insert the table using the Insert Table dialog box
- Draw a table
- Convert text to table
- Create a quick table
- Construct a table from an Excel worksheet.

How to create a Table by Dragging the Table Menu

You can create a table by dragging the table menu. To do this, follow the steps below

- Select the **Insert** tab and click on **Table** in the **Table** group

Figure 130: Insert table

- A drop-down menu is open containing a grid. Hover over the **Grid** to select the numbers of columns and rows you want.

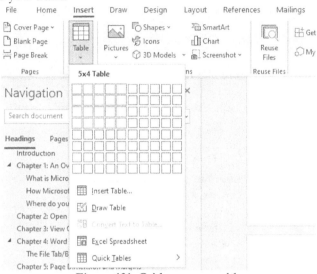

Figure 131: Grid to create table

- Click on the **Grid**, release your mouse, and the table will appear.

Inserting the Table Using the Insert Table Dialog Box

Another way to create a table is by using the Insert Table dialog box. To insert a table using the Insert Table dialog box, follow the steps given below:

- Go to the **Insert** tab and click on **Table** in the **Table** group

- In the drop-down menu, click on **Insert Table**

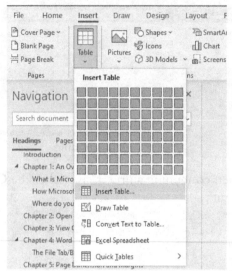

Figure 132: Insert Table Dialog Box

- In the Insert Table dialog box, enter the number of columns and rows and how you want the column to **Autofit.**

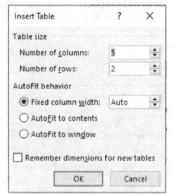

Figure 133: Insert Table Dialog Box Autofit

- Then click on **Ok.**

Tables give you a convenient way to display information that might otherwise be bulky and confusing.

EDITING A TABLE

The following will explain how to edit your table.

Inserting Rows and Columns

To Insert Rows and Columns;

- Move the cursor to the row or column you want adjacent to the reference. This selects the table, and the **Table Design and Layout** tabs appear.

- Select the **Layout** tab.

- Choose **Insert Above, Insert Below,** or **Insert Left** or **Insert Right** depending on where you want the new row or column.

Figure 134: Editing your table

Movement within a Table
To move within your table

What to do	What it does
To select an entire table	Go to the top left corner of a table and click on the table move handle.
To select an entire column	Drag over the column's content or Click the column top border.
To select an entire row	Drag over the row's content or Place your mouse pointer on the left margin pointing to your desired row and click.
To select a single cell	Drag over the cell's content or click thrice inside the cell.
Keyboard Arrow Keys	Arrow keys will move up and down, left and right.
Tab	The **Tab** key is used to move from left to right.
Shift + Tab	Use **Shift +Tab** to move from right to left.

Adjusting Column Width

To adjust column width;
Columns in a newly added table have the same width. However, sometimes there's the need to change the column width to accommodate the data entered.

Using the mouse:
- Place your mouse pointer on the column boundary—the mouse pointer changes to a double vertical line with the left and right arrows.

- Drag the mouse pointer to the direction you want to change the width.

- Release the mouse button when you are satisfied with the width size.

Using AutoFit:
AutoFit in Word is a feature that will automatically adjust your column width to accommodate the widest text entered in any table column. It is more advisable to **AutoFit** the entire table.
- Place your mouse pointer at the left-most column boundary; the mouse pointer appears as a double vertical line with the left and right arrows.

- Double-click on the mouse button.

Using the Table Tools:
- Click in the cell within the column to be resized.

- Click the **Layout** tab.

- In the **Width** box, click on the up (increase) or down (decrease) arrow to change the width.

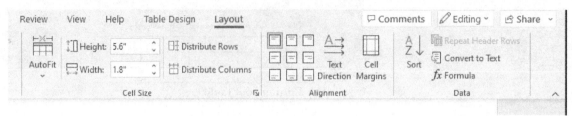

Figure 135: Using table tools

Merge Cells, Split Cells, or Table
To Merge Cells, Split Cells, or Table;
To merge cells means to combine two or more adjacent cells to form a single cell. Splitting cells is the opposite.

- Select the cells you want to merge or split or all the cells in the table boundary you want to split.

- Click **Layout.**

- Click **Merge Cells, Split Cells, or Split Table,** depending on your task.

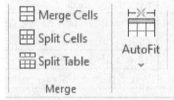

Figure 136: Merging or splitting table

Delete Cells, Rows, Columns, or Table
You may want to delete a Cell, Row, Column, or Table from your document.
To Delete Cells, Rows, Columns, and Table;
- Select the cell or cells to be deleted.

- Click the **Layout** tab.

- Click the **Delete** button. The delete options will appear.

- Choose from the available options the task you want to perform.

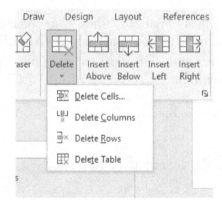

Figure 137: Table deletion actions

DRAWING A TABLE

While working with a table, you might want to add cells within a table or when you know your table is not going to be uniform.

To draw a table;

- Go to **insert**.

- Click **Tables**.

- Select **Draw Tables**. Your mouse pointer turns into a pencil tool, and you can draw within your document.

- Drag your mouse into your desired size and shape before releasing **it. Alternatively;**

- Click within the table in your document.

- Click the **Table Design** tab.

- Select **Draw Tables**.

ERASING PART OF A TABLE

To erase part of a table;

- Click within the table in your document.

- Click the **Table Design** tab.

- Select **Eraser.** Your mouse pointer turns into an eraser.

- Place your mouse over the table line to be removed.

- Drag the mouse over the line to erase. The line appears selected before you release your mouse.

- Release your mouse to erase the line.

- Repeat for as many lines as you want.

- When you are done, click **Esc**.

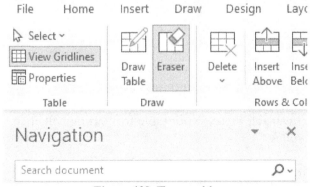

Figure 138: Erase table

FORMATTING A TABLE

While working with tables in Microsoft Word, it has several built-in table styles you can to your table for quick and consistent formatting or creates your own.

Gridline

Gridlines are borders that appear in your document when you add them while working with tables. Therefore, when working with tables, it is always advisable to put them on. Gridlines only appear as a format in your document but do not print.

To Turn On your Gridlines;

- Click within the table in your document.

- Click the **Layout** tab.

- Click **View Gridlines**. Gridlines will appear for all word documents.

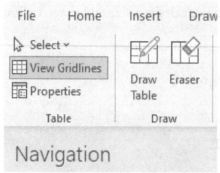

Figure 139: View gridlines

Applying Table Styles

Applying the same style to all the tables is advisable when working with multiple tables. Using the table styles rather than manually applying style to each table or direct formatting can be done. It ensures consistent formatting of your tables and saves a lot of time.

To apply a table style;

- Click within the table in your document.

- Click the **Table Design** tab.

- Click the More down arrow in the Table Styles for more styles, as shown below.

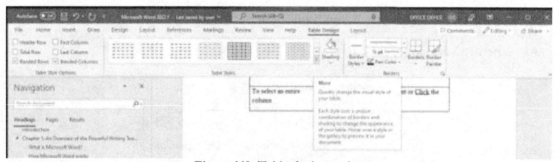

Figure 140: Table design styles

- Select from the available styles. Your table formatting will change as you hover over different table styles.

- Click your desired style to apply to your table.

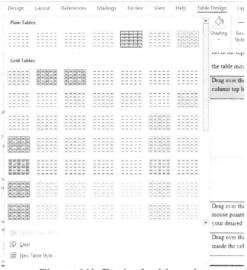

Figure 141: Desired table styles

Selecting Table Style Options

After applying your table style, there are different table options for you to select from it. These options affect the table style format.

To select Table Style Options;

- Click within the table in your document.

- Click the **Table Design** tab.

- Go to **Table Style Options**

- **Header Row**: If checked, the header row, i.e., the first row in a table containing headings for all columns, will be formatted differently from the body rows.
- **Total Row**: If checked, it will format the last row differently from the body rows. E.g., to create a row for mathematical totals.
- **Banded Rows/Columns**: If checked, format even and odd rows differently. There's alternate row/column shading, so they are easier to read.
- **First or the Last Column**: If checked, the first or last column is formatted differently from the other columns.

Figure 142: Table style options

The Table below has the above Table Styles Options

Name	Class ID	Subject

Modifying a Table Style

A style can be modified after applying it to a table. Once modified, the change will reflect all tables using that style.

To modify a table style;
- Click within the table in your document.

- Click the **Table Design** tab.

- Click the More down arrow in the Table Styles.

- Click **Modify Table Style** or Right Click a table style and select **Modify**; a dialogue box appears.

- Modify your formatting, i.e., font size, style, color, fills, etc.

- Select;

- **Only in this document** if the modified style is applied to only the current document.
- **New Documents based on this template** for the style to be modified for future documents based on the current template.
- Click **OK.**

 Note: A manually or directly applied table style will likely override a modified style. If you apply a table style and the tables using that style do not change, that might be the reason. You may then need to clear the formatting before the change is applied.
Below is the Modify Style Dialog box

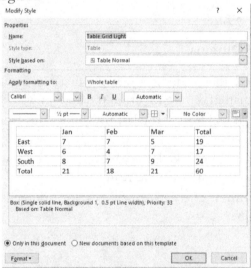

Figure 143: Modifying table style

Modifying Table Properties in a Table Style
Table properties, including cell margin, row settings, and table alignment, can be modified using **Format** in the **Modify Style.**
To change Table Properties in a Table Style;
- Click within the table in your document.

- Click the **Table Design** tab.

- Click the More down arrow in the Table Styles.

- Click **Modify Table Style** or Right Click a table style and select **Modify**; a dialogue box appears.

- Click **Format** on the bottom left of the dialogue box. A dropdown menu appears with several options.

- Click the option you want to modify; a dialogue box appears with other options.

Figure 144: Modifying table properties

- Click on the **Table Properties** option, the dialogue box below.

- Select any formatting option you want to apply to your table.

- Click **OK.**

- Select whether to apply **Only in this document** or **New documents based on this template.**

- Click **OK.**

Creating a New Table Style

If you don't want to use the already built-in table styles, you can create a new or custom style for your use.

To create a custom table style;

- Click within the table in your document.

- Click the **Table Design** tab.

- Click the More down arrow in the Table Styles.

- Select a table style to apply as a base style.

- Click the More down arrow in the Table Styles.

- Click **New Table Style, and** a dialog box appears.

- Name a name for the new table in the Name box.

- Format your table accordingly.

- Select whether to apply **Only in this document** or **New documents based on this template.**

- Click **OK.**

The new style appears in the Table styles gallery under **Custom** at the top. Just right-click on the style and select Delete Table Style to delete it.

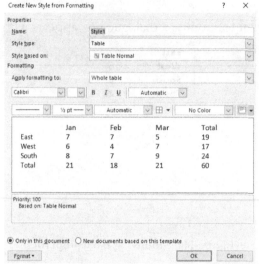

Figure 145: Creating a new custom table style

Clearing a Table Style

This is to clear a table style and remove formatting;

- Click within the table in your document.

- Click the **Table Design** tab.

- Click the More down arrow in the Table Styles.

- Click **Clear.**

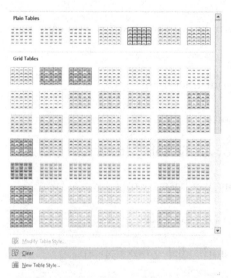

Figure 146: Clear a table style

Setting a Default Table Style

Setting a default table style means applying that style for new tables in the current document or all new documents that will come after the setting.

To set a Default Table Style;

- Click within the table in your document.

- Click the **Table Design** tab.

- Click the More down arrow in the Table Styles.

- Then right-Click the table style to be used as the default style.

- Select Set as Default from the drop-down menu. A dialogue box appears.

- Select from the options.

- Click **OK**.

14.3 Caption Insertion & Updating

Captions are labels like "Figure 1" added to objects like figures, tables, or equations. They help in organizing and referencing objects in your document. Here's how to work with them:

Adding Captions:

1. Click on the object (could be a table, figure, equation, etc.) you want to label.

2. Go to the References tab and click on Insert Caption in the Captions section.

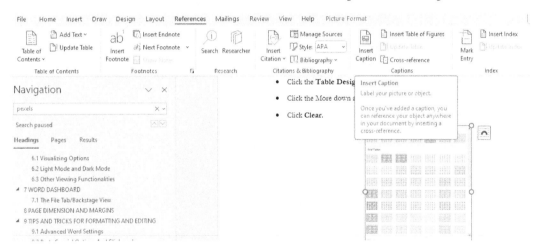

Figure 147: Inserting captions

3. Choose the appropriate label from the Label list. If your desired label isn't there, click New Label, type it in, and hit OK.

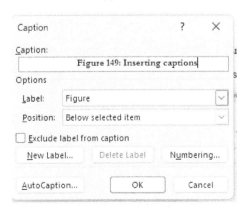

Figure 148: Appropriate label in a caption

4. Add any extra text you want after the label.

5. Click OK.

Automatic Captions:

Word can automatically label objects as you insert them.

1. Click on the object you want to label.

2. Under the References tab, click Insert Caption.

3. In the dialog box that appears, click AutoCaption.

4. Check the boxes for the objects you want Word to label automatically. You can also pick where you want the label to appear using the Position list.

Updating Caption Numbers:

If you add or remove a caption, you'll want to update the numbering.

1. Highlight any of the captions in your document.

2. Right-click and choose Update Field. This will refresh all caption numbers.

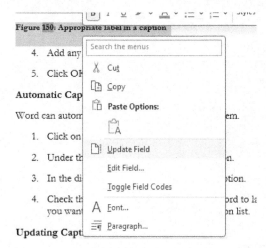

Figure 149: Updating Captions

Formatting Captions:

After adding a caption, you'll see a "Caption" style in the style gallery.

1. To change the look of all captions, right-click the "Caption" style and select Modify.

2. Adjust font, size, color, and more.

Deleting Captions:

1. Click on the caption you want to remove.

2. Press the Delete key.

3. If you have other captions, update them by pressing CTRL+A and then F9. This ensures correct numbering after removal.

14.4 Copyright & Image Selection

Copyrights:

When you're working on a document, especially in a professional setting, it's essential to understand the importance of copyright. Copyright is a law that gives the creator of a work (like a book, movie, picture, song, or website) the right to say how other people can use it. Copyright laws are the rules that govern how authors and publishers distribute, sell and use their work. These laws protect authors and publishers who have created original works. For more information, check out Wikipedia. So, if you're using someone else's picture or drawing in your Word document, you need to be sure you have the right to do so.

Now, imagine you're working on a report for your boss. You find the perfect image online. It's tempting to just copy and paste it into your document. But wait! That image might be copyrighted. Using it without permission could get you and your company in trouble.

Image copyright free/public domain:

Image copyright-free indicates images that are free of any copyright restrictions. This means that every person can use the pictures without having to pay or get permission from any other person who owns the copyright of the picture.

There are many places online where you can find images that are free to use. Websites like Pixabay or Unsplash offer pictures that creators have said anyone can use, even for business. But always check the rules on each website. Some might ask you to give the artist credit.

Image copyright free/public domain can be found in the following sources:

- Flickr.com, a marketplace for images and art created by the community
- Pexels.com, commercial-free stock photos from different sources all over the world.
- Pixabay.com is a growing collection of public domain photos uploaded by users and can be used for free under their CC0 license.
- Depositphotos.com is an excellent illustration stock photography and illustrations free of copyright restrictions.

But what if you're set on using a specific image that's copyrighted? You might be able to buy a license. This means you pay to use the picture. Websites like Shutterstock or Getty Images let you do this. Remember, buying a license doesn't mean you own the image. It means you've got permission to use it in a certain way.

Another thing to think about is the quality of the image. If you're printing your Word document, you'll want a high-quality image. It should be clear, not blurry. In Word, you can change the size of an image, but making it too big might make it look fuzzy. Always try to find the best quality image for your needs.

Now, let's talk about selecting images. Choose pictures that match your topic. If you're writing about dogs, don't use a picture of a cat. It might confuse your readers. Also, think about the mood of your document. If it's a serious report, don't use a silly picture. But if it's a fun announcement, a playful image might be perfect.

In Word, adding an image is easy. Go to the Insert tab and click on Pictures. You can choose a file from your computer. Once it's in your document, you can move it, resize it, and even add some styles to it. Play around with the options to see what looks best.

Remember, images can make your document look great. But always think about copyright. It's better to be safe than sorry. And always choose images that help tell your story. They should add to your words, not distract from them.

In the end, copyright might seem like a tricky topic. But it's all about respect. Artists work hard to create images. Just like you work hard on your Word documents. So, always use images in a way that respects the artist's wishes. And if you're ever unsure, it's a good idea to ask for help. Maybe someone at your company knows about copyright. Or you could even ask a lawyer. It's always better to be safe than sorry.

Royalty-free or Creative Commons:

Creative Commons is an organization that provides tools for copyright-free material to be shared and distributed on the internet and applies certain conditions regarding these sharing rights. This means that the usage of the material can be flexible. However, the third party who wants to use this material must agree to the terms of use and license agreement.

Inserting Copyright, Trademark, and Registered Symbols in Word

Microsoft Word has many special characters. Three common ones are the copyright, trademark, and registered symbols. Here's how to add them to your document.

Using the Symbol Dialog Box

This method uses Word's built-in Symbol dialog box.

1. Click where you want the symbol.
2. Go to the Insert tab.
3. Click on Symbol.
4. Choose More Symbols.
5. Click on the Special Characters tab.
6. Pick Copyright, Registered, or Trademark.
7. Click Insert.
8. Close the Symbol box.

Using Keyboard Shortcuts

If you're on a PC, use these shortcuts:

1. Click where you want the symbol.
2. Use the right key combo:
   - Copyright: Alt + Ctrl + C
   - Trademark: Alt + Ctrl + T
   - Registered: Alt + Ctrl + R

Using AutoCorrect

Word's AutoCorrect can also add these symbols.

1. Click where you want the symbol.
2. Type the right combo:
   - Copyright: (c)
   - Registered: (r)
   - Trademark: (tm)

Tip: If AutoCorrect doesn't work, check if it's on. Go to File, then Options, then Proofing, and then AutoCorrect Options. Keep an eye on this blog for more tips on using AutoCorrect in Word.

15 THE GRAPHS AND CHARTS

When you think of Microsoft Word, you might picture typing up reports or crafting letters. But Word isn't just about words. It's also about presenting data in a way that's easy to understand. That's where graphs and charts come in.

What's a Graph? A graph is like a picture. It shows data in a visual way. Think of when you've seen the weather forecast. Those lines that go up and down? That's a graph. It helps you see if it's getting warmer or cooler over time.

And a Chart? A chart is a bit different. It's also a picture of data. But it might show parts of a whole. Like, if you had 10 apples and ate 2, a chart could show that you ate a part of all the apples you had. Graphs and charts offer a visual representation of data, making it simpler to interpret and understand. Microsoft Word provides a variety of options for inserting these visuals into your document. Here's a comprehensive guide on how to do it:

Types of Graphs and Charts

There are many types of graphs and charts. Some of the most common ones are:

1. **Bar Graph**: Represents data using bars or strips, either horizontally or vertically. It's commonly used in business and financial analysis. The taller the bar, the bigger the number it represents.
2. **Line Graph**: This uses lines to show data over time. Displays quantitative data over a specific time interval, typically with two axes: the x-axis (horizontal) and the y-axis (vertical). It's like watching a path that goes up and down.
3. **Pie Chart**: Represents data in the form of pie slices, showcasing parts of a whole. This is a circle cut into pieces. Each piece shows a part of a whole.
4. **Scatter Plot**: An XY plot that showcases the relationship between two sets of data. This shows dots on a graph. It can help see if two things are related.

INSERTING A CHART INTO YOUR DOCUMENT

A chart is another Word feature that lets you virtually present your information or data. You can insert any chart in your Word document.

To insert a chart in your document:

1. Place your insertion point where you want the chart.
2. Go to the **Insert** ribbon.
3. Click **Chart** in the **Illustration** group.

Insert Chart dialog box appears.

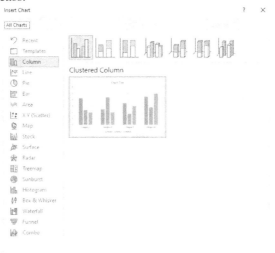

Figure 150: Insert chart dialog box

4. Select a chart type and double-click on the desired chart.

The chart appears in your document with an excel spreadsheet.

5. Input your data into the excel spreadsheet, and the charts update your data.
6. Close the spreadsheet window.

FORMATTING A CHART

1. Select the chart.
2. Click on the plus sign at the top right corner.
3. Check or uncheck the box of elements to put or remove them from the chart.
4. Click on the arrow in front of any selected elements for more settings.
5. Click on the **More Option** to have control of the element from the element Format dialog box.

Each element has its **Format** dialog box to format your chart elements fully. You can change their color, width, size, gap, etc., as the case may be. The format dialog box can also be opened by:

- Double-clicking on the element or

- Right-clicking on the element and choosing **Format Data Series** from the list of the options or

- Using the keyboard shortcut command **Ctrl + 1** on the element.

You can also format your chart in the contextual **Chart Tools** tap (Design and Format buttons) or at the brush icon ![brush], the chart style below the **+** sign. You can filter your chart using the chart filter ![filter] below the chart style icon.

Figure 151: Adding Graphs

Creating a Bar Graph

Want to make a bar graph in Word? Here's how:

1. Open your Word document.
2. Position your cursor where you'd like the bar graph.
3. Navigate to the 'Insert' tab and select 'Chart' from the 'Illustrations' group.
4. In the 'Insert Chart' dialog box, choose 'Bar' from the left panel. Pick the specific bar chart style and click 'OK'.
5. Now you can add your data!

Inserting a Line Graph

Line graphs are great for showing changes. Here's how to make one:

1. Open your Word document.
2. Click where you want to place your graph in the document.
3. Navigate to the 'Insert' tab and select 'Chart' from the 'Illustrations' group.
4. In the 'Insert Chart' dialog box, choose 'Line' from the left panel. Select your preferred line graph style and click 'OK'.

5. Add your data and, you are set!

Creating a Scatter Plot

Scatter plots are cool for comparing things. Here's how to create one:

1. Open your Word document.
2. Click where you want to the graph in your document.
3. Navigate to the 'Insert' tab and select 'Chart' from the 'Illustrations' group.
4. In the 'Insert Chart' dialog box, choose 'XY (Scatter)' from the left panel. Pick your desired scatter plot style and click 'OK'.
5. Add your data.

Inserting a Pie Chart

Pie charts show parts of a whole. Like slices of a pie. Here's how to make one:

1. Open your Word document.
2. Position your cursor where you'd like the pie chart.
3. Navigate to the 'Insert' tab and click on 'Chart' in the 'Illustrations' group.
4. In the 'Insert Chart' dialog box, select 'Pie'. Choose the specific pie chart style you want and click 'OK'.
5. Add your data and you are good to go!

Remember, after inserting any graph or chart, Word will also open an Excel window. This allows you to input or modify the data that the graph or chart will display. Once you've made your changes in Excel, simply close it, and Word will automatically update the graph or chart with the new data.

16 COMMON PROBLEMS AND MISTAKES

Microsoft Word is a powerful tool. But like any tool, sometimes things can go wrong. We've all been there. You're working on a big report, and suddenly something doesn't look right. Or worse, you can't find your file at all! Let's talk about some common problems and how to fix them.

Temporary Files: What Are They?

When you work in Word, it makes a copy of your file. This copy is called a temporary file. It's like a backup. If Word closes suddenly, this file can help you get your work back.

But sometimes, these files can cause problems. Maybe you can't open your document. Or Word keeps freezing. Often, the temporary file is the reason.

How to Deal with Temporary Files

1. First, close Word. Make sure it's not running.
2. Next, go to the folder where your file is. Look for a file that starts with "~". This is the temporary file.
3. Delete this file. Don't worry; it's just a copy.
4. Now, open Word again. Your document should work fine.

Retrieve a draft

Despite your best efforts to preserve your Word documents, a computer breakdown or power outage may prevent you from saving the most recent version of your work. If that happens, don't worry. Word may have saved it as a draft using the Automatic Repair feature.

- To find the draft, go to File > Open.

- Select Recent Documents.

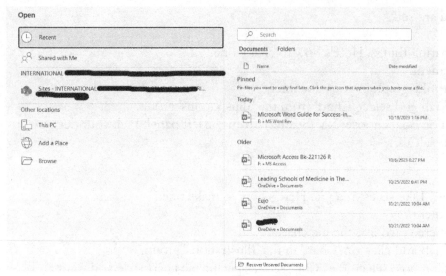

Figure 152: Recent documents

- Scroll to the bottom of your recent paper's list. The Recover Unsaved Documents button is located at the bottom.
- Press the button.
- The dialog box Open will display. Select the document to be recovered, then click the Open button.

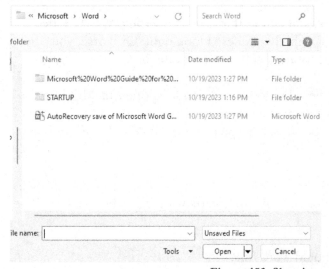

Figure 153: Showing any unsaved copies

Autosave Settings: A Lifesaver!

Have you ever lost your work because Word closed? It's frustrating. But there's a feature that can help. It's called Autosave.

Autosave saves your work every few minutes. So, if something goes wrong, you won't lose much.

Setting Up Autosave

1. Open Word.
2. Go to 'File' and then 'Options'.
3. Click on 'Save' on the left side.
4. Look for 'Save AutoRecover information'. Make sure it's checked.
5. Next to it, you can choose how often to save. Every 10 minutes is a good choice.

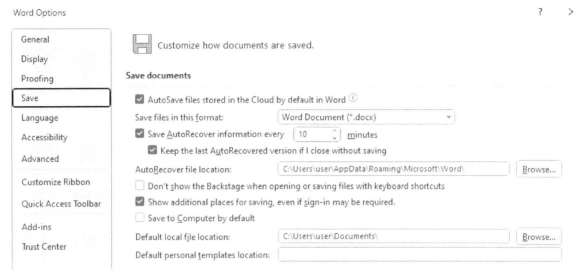

Figure 154: Autorecover settings

6. Click 'OK'. Now, Word will save your work automatically.

AUTOSAVE WITH AUTO RECOVER

Word has AutoRecover to recover the unsaved files, but it may not fail you if you fail to set it up accurately. To set AutoRecover to save the unsaved file, kindly;

1. Tap on the **File and select Option** from the backstage to open the Word Options dialog box.
2. Select **Save,** then choose **Save AutoRecover Information,** and **set the minutes** you want MS word to continue saving the document for you automatically.
3. Tap **Ok** and **close** the dialog box.

Figure 155: Autosave settings

But My File Is Still Gone!

Sometimes, even with Autosave, things go wrong. Maybe your computer turned off. Or Word had an error. But don't panic. There's still hope.

1. Open Word.
2. Go to 'File' and then 'Info'.
3. Look for 'Manage Document'. Click on it.
4. Choose 'Recover Unsaved Documents'.
5. A new window will open. Here, you'll see files that Word saved. Look for your file.
6. Click on it and then 'Open'. Your file should be back!

A Few More Tips

1. Always save your work often. Don't rely just on Autosave.
2. Make a backup of important files. Save them in another place, like a USB drive.

3. If Word is acting strange, restart it. Sometimes, that's all it needs.

PROTECTING YOUR DOCUMENT

The best means of restricting frustration is to adequately secure the document from other people, most times if it is a family or joint desktop. To create secure your document to a greater level, do well to:

1. Tap on **the File** and select **Info** from backstage.

2. Tap on **Protect document menu and** select the **best option** preferable to you.

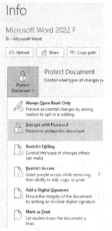

Figure 156: Protecting your document

3. Supply the required information regarding the option you selected and tap Ok.

Figure 157: Protecting your document with a password

Note: take caution with whatever option you select. If you are locked out of the document, you have no other option but to re-access the document.

16.1 Avoiding Common Microsoft Word Pitfalls

Microsoft Word is packed with tools to make your writing shine. But sometimes, these tools can trip you up if you don't use them right. Let's dive into some common mistakes people make in Word and how to steer clear of them.

1. **Indenting with Spaces or Tabs** It's tempting to use the space bar or tab key to create indents. But this can mess up your document's look. If you change anything, those indents might shift and throw everything off.

How to Fix It Instead of pressing space or tab:

- Go to the "Home" tab and click the small arrow in the "Paragraph" section.
- Under "Indentation," pick "First line" from the "Special" menu.
- Choose how deep you want your indent to be next to "By."
- Hit "OK" to save. If you want this for all new documents, click "Set As Default."

2. **Double Tapping Enter After Paragraphs** Some folks press "Enter" twice to make a gap between paragraphs. But if you change your document later, these gaps might end up in weird places.

How to Fix It For a neat space between paragraphs:
- Highlight the text you want to change.
- In the "Home" tab, go to "Paragraph." Click "Line and Paragraph Spacing," then pick "Add Space Before Paragraph."

3. **Ignoring the Spelling and Grammar Tool** Word has a tool that spots spelling and grammar mistakes. But some people turn it off because the red and blue lines bother them. If you do this, you might miss some errors.

How to Fix It Keep the spelling and grammar tool on:
- Go to the "Review" tab and click "Editor."
- If you want to pick which errors it finds, go to "File," then "Options," and finally "Proofing."

4. **Changing Text Styles One by One** Word has lots of ways to change how your text looks. You might change each word's style by hand. But this takes ages. And if you want to change a style later, you have to find and fix every single bit of text.

How to Fix It Use the "Styles" options in the "Home" tab. Pick a style and apply it to your text. This way, your document looks neat, and changing styles is a breeze.

Some More Microsoft Word Troubles? Here's Your Fix!

Microsoft Word is a favorite tool for many. But like all software, it can sometimes act up. Don't worry! Microsoft is always on the lookout to squash those pesky bugs. Let's dive into some common Word hiccups and how to tackle them.

Common Word Glitches

1. Trouble Opening a Word File
2. "Microsoft Word Has Stopped Working" Alert
3. Constant Word Crashes
4. Word Freezes Up
5. Word File Seems Broken

Glitch 1: Can't Open That Word File?

Sometimes, you might see an error saying, "Word had trouble opening the file." This can happen if another app messed with your Word file.

How to Fix It?

Method 1: Let the File In
- Right-click the problematic Word file.
- Choose Properties.
- Click Unblock, then OK.

Method 2: Trust Your File
- Move the tricky Word file to a new spot.
- Open Word, click File, then Options.
- Go to Trust Center, then Trust Center Settings.
- Pick Trusted Locations, then Add new location.
- Choose where you moved your Word file. Click OK.

Glitch 2: Word's Taking a Nap

Seeing "Microsoft Word Has Stopped Working"? Sometimes other apps or outdated drivers can cause this.

How to Fix It?

Method 1: Freshen Up Word
- Open Word, click File, then Account.
- Click Update Options, then Update Now.

Method 2: Check on Add-ins
- Press Windows Key + R.
- Type winword /safe and press OK.
- If Word's good in safe mode, the add-ins might be the issue. Turn them off one by one to find the culprit.

Glitch 3: Word's Being Clumsy

Does Word crash a lot? Or does it say, "Sorry, Word's having trouble"? This can be due to many reasons.

How to Fix It?

Method 1: Check on Office

- Go to Windows Settings, then Apps.
- Find Microsoft Office or Word. Click Modify.
- Choose Quick Repair or Online Repair. Follow the steps.

Glitch 4: Word's Stuck

Is Word not responding? This can be due to many reasons like bad settings or a messy install.

How to Fix It?

Method 1: Reinstall Word

- Go to Control Panel, then Programs.
- Find Microsoft Word. Click Uninstall.
- After it's gone, reinstall Word.

Method 2: Fix Word

If reinstalling didn't help, Word might be broken.

- Follow the steps in Glitch 3, Method 1 to repair Word.

17 TABLE OF CONTENTS, IMAGE LIST, TABLE LIST, INDEX

MAKING A TABLE OF CONTENTS

The table of contents serves as a guide to each topic you discussed in the textbook. When you prepare the table of contents, the table of contents will have a number page with each heading and subheading, provided you have numbered your document. The style that will be used for preparing the table of contents is the style. For example, heading 1 is for the chapter number and main heading. In addition, you may use headings 2 and 3 for sub-heading. If you use the heading style correctly, you won't have a problem preparing a table of contents. To create a table of contents, follow this simple guide:

1. Create a style for chapter, heading, and subheading with heading 1, 2, or 3.

2. Move to the beginning of the document and place the cursor pointer at the beginning of the first paragraph.

3. Then tap on the **Insert tab** and select the **blank page** from the page section to create a separate blank page for the table of contents at the beginning of the document.

4. Place the cursor pointer on the blank page and move to the **References tab.**

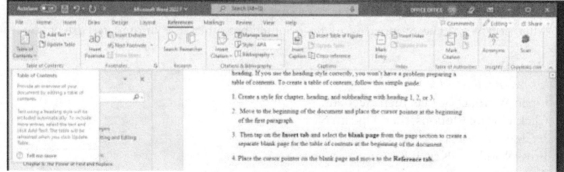

Figure 158: References tab

5. Move to the table of contents section and tap on the "**table of content**" menu button.

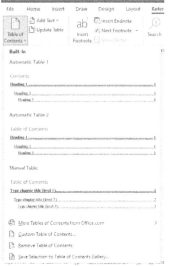

Figure 159: Table of contents options

6. Select a **preferred table of contents format** for your document; immediately after you select the format, a table of contents will be created.

Table of Contents

Introduction 5

Chapter 1: An Overview of the Powerful Writing Tool - Microsoft Word 2022 8

What is Microsoft Word? 8

How Microsoft Word works 9

Where do you buy Microsoft Word? 9

Chapter 2: Open a blank document or an existing template 13

Chapter 3: View options 19

Chapter 4: Word Dashboard 26

The File Tab/Backstage View 32

Chapter 5: Page dimension and margins 44

Chapter 6: Tips and Tricks For Formatting and Editing 47

Figure 160: Sample table of contents

Note: if you added an item to the table of contents by attaching more heading styles, update it to the table of contents by tapping on the Update table under the contents section, then select how to update it and tap Ok.

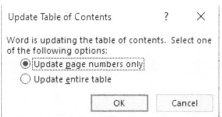

Figure 161: Update table of contents

Microsoft Word has a feature that enables you to generate a table of content automatically or manually with easy-to-use templates. To insert a table of contents automatically in your document, you must create or format your document using the Word built-in headings in the **Styles** group

To Insert a Table of Contents:

1. Ensure your document headings uses Word built-in headings styles

2. Place your insertion point where you want the table of content to be.
3. Go to the **References** ribbon.
4. Click **Table of Contents**.

A drop-down menu appears.

5. Select an option:

- The first two options automatically insert your table of contents with **all** your available headings.

- The third option inserts the table of contents with placeholder texts and allows you to replace them with your headings.

- Select **More Tables of Contents from Office.com** for more templates.

- Select the **Custom Table of Content** to customize your table. A dialog box appears; edit as desired, and press **OK**.

- If you already have a table of content in your document, you can delete it by selecting **Remove Table of Contents.**

Updating your Table of Contents

Word does not update your table of content automatically if you make changes to your document. You will have to update it manually.

To update your Table of Content:

1. Position your cursor in the table of content.

Table borders appear with buttons at the top-left.

2. Click the **Update Table** button.

A dialog box appears.

3. Click the **Update entire table**.

4. Press **OK**.

Word automatically updates your table.

Alternatively,

1. Right-click on the table of content.

A drop-down menu appears.

2. Select **Update Field.** You can also select **Update Table** in the **Table of Contents** group in the **References** ribbon.

A dialog box appears.

3. Click **Update the entire table.**

4. Click **OK**.

Note: Do not always forget to update your table after making significant changes that affect the headers or page numbers.

CREATING AN INDEX

An index is just like the table of contents, but the index goes deeper than the table of contents. The index gives clues to every item of importance in the document. To create an index, these are the route paths:

1. Select the word or group of words that you want to include in the index list

2. Tap on the **Reference tab** and move to the index group, then tap on the **Mark entry button** to open the Mark Index Entry dialog box.

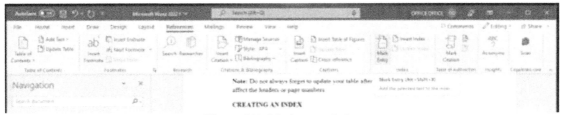

Figure 162: Mark entry index

3. Mark entry dialog box will be opened with the selected text in the main entry. In addition, you may insert a subentry for more explanation about the main entry.

4. Click **Mark or Mark all button. T**he mark is to mark only the selected item, while the **Mark is to mark all the items that match** the selected item in the document.

5. Mark all the items you want to be included in the index list inside the document and close the Mark index entry dialog box.

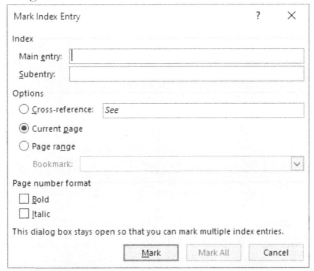

Figure 163: Mark entry index creation

6. Close the show/hide command by tapping the **show/hide button** in **the Home tab** in the Paragraph section. The show/hide command is used to show itself automatically immediately after you mark any index entry.

Figure 164: Show hide index button

7. Place the cursor pointer where you want to put the index list, which is proper to appear at the end of the note.

8. Tap on the **Reference tab** and the **Insert Index button** at the index section to open an Index dialog box.

Figure 165: Insert index button

9. Make the necessary settings, such as style index in format, number of columns you want to create for the Index in the column section, and the page alignment.

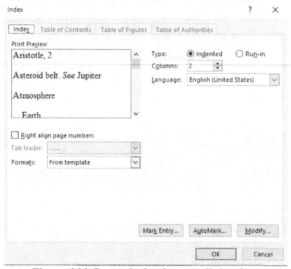

Figure 166: Insert index button dialog box

10. When you are done with the setting, tap on **Ok** to Insert the Index list into the document.

Note: Heading and subheading have to be in the Index list. You have to get them added. You can delete and amend the index if you are not pleased with the arrangement by commanding for insert index dialog box.

CREATING A LIST OF FIGURES

A "List of Figures" is mainly used to create a list of tables you caption. If you fail to prepare a caption for each table you have in the document, a "List of Figures" will not work. To create a "list of the figure," do well to:

- Tap on the **References tab** and move to the captions section.

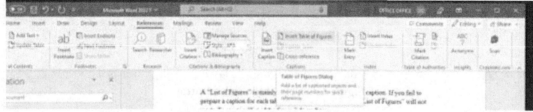

Figure 167: Insert table of figures

- Then click on **Insert Table of the figure** to open the table of the figure dialog box.

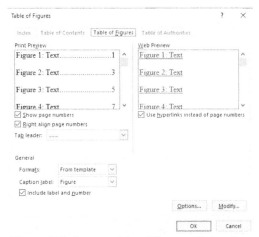

Figure 168: Insert table of figures dialog box

- But you must have created a caption for the table you have in the document.

Figure 169: List of figures

INSERTING AUTOMATIC TABLE OF FIGURES

Word has a command to automatically add a table of figures to your work, just like adding a table of contents.

To automatically generate a table of figures, you must have added captions to all the figures used in your document using the Word **Insert Caption** command.

To Insert Table of Figures:

1. Ensure you use the Word caption feature to add captions to your objects.
2. Place your insertion point where you want the table of figures to be.
3. Click the **References** tab.
4. Select **Insert Table of Figures** in the **Caption** group. Table of Figures dialog box appears.
5. Select your desired Format, make other changes, preview, and press **OK**. Your table of figures appears in your document.

FOOTNOTES AND ENDNOTES

Footnotes and endnotes contain additional notes to supplement and explain ahead of what is mentioned in the text. Footnotes will be inserted at the bottom of the page, while the Endnote will be inserted at the end of the chapter, section, and document. To make footnotes or endnotes, do well to:

1. Select the word or the group of words that you want to reference with a footnote or endnote.
2. Tap the **references tab** and select either the **footnote or endnote.**

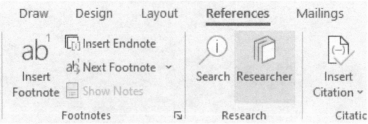
Figure 170: Footnotes and endnotes

3. Type the **footnote or endnote** at the provided place where the command transit you in the document with the superscripted number.

---

[1] Designing footnotes|

Figure 171: Footnote sample

Note: check the footnote and endnote information by clicking the superscripted number on the document's reference word (s).

| endnote information [1]
Figure 172: Footnote wrapping text

Tip: You can check the footnote and endnote as they are arranged in the document by tapping on show notes. Once you delete the reference text, the footnote and Endnote will be deleted as well

18 ERROR CHECKS

No matter how perfect and flawless you are on Word, there will always be some unavoidable mistakes or errors that occur around spelling and grammar. These errors can cost you more than you imagine, especially in business and education. To avoid these errors, that is why you need to make the best use of the Proofing Tools.

18.1 Grammar Revising

USING AUTOCORRECT IN WORD

AutoCorrect is a function found in all Microsoft products that allows you to change how words are spelled or shown in your documents, and it comes preloaded with several options.

Autocorrect is one of the amazing features of Word that fixes hundreds of common spelling errors and typos automatically. Moreover, the correction happens instantly, and you might not even notice it. For instance, you cannot type the word **help** because Word automatically corrects it to **help** by default. Let's imagine you want to spell out the word "the," but you misspelled it slightly; pressing the spacebar will automatically change it to "the." Likewise, if you type "acn" and press space, Word detects that you're probably trying to spell "can," but you've just misspelled it, automatically changing it for you. That is an autocorrect option; it will detect or recognize often misspelled words and correct them for you, which is a beneficial tool. It will also help with other subjects, such as fractions. For example, if you were typing half (1/2), pressing the space bar turns it to that fraction; similarly, if you were typing 1/4, using the spacebar converts it to that fraction. Again, Word's autocorrect option is being used. Aside from typos and spelling errors, autocorrect features helps in fixing common punctuation mistakes, automatically capitalizing the first letter of any sentence, names of days, months, and some inverse capitalization errors. Ordinals are another example; you might see them in things like dates. For example, if you type the 1st of August and press the spacebar, the "st" becomes a superscript, bringing the date into proper format; the same goes for the 2nd, and so on. Another example would be

Hyperlinks. If you write in a website address and hit Enter, it will highlight the website and turn it into a hyperlink, which you can see by hovering over it. If you hold down the Ctrl key and click your mouse, it will take you to that website. This is where the autocorrect choices come in handy.

Let's look at several other autocorrect features, one of which is quite a cute little one if you've never seen it before. If you **input three dashes** (---) and **press Enter**, you'll get a continuous solid line, and the best part is that you can go up and type on the line if you want to.

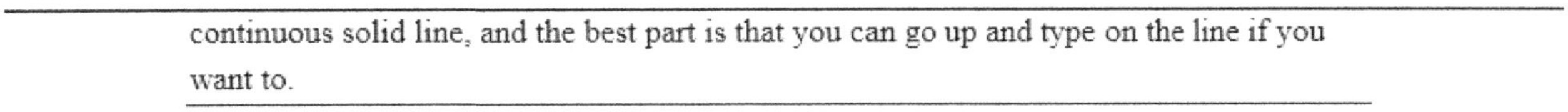

continuous solid line, and the best part is that you can go up and type on the line if you want to.

Figure 173: Three dashes

You get a solid bold line if you do that again, but this time you **hold down your shift key**, do **three dashes**, and hit **Enter**; you just incorporate the shift to get that.

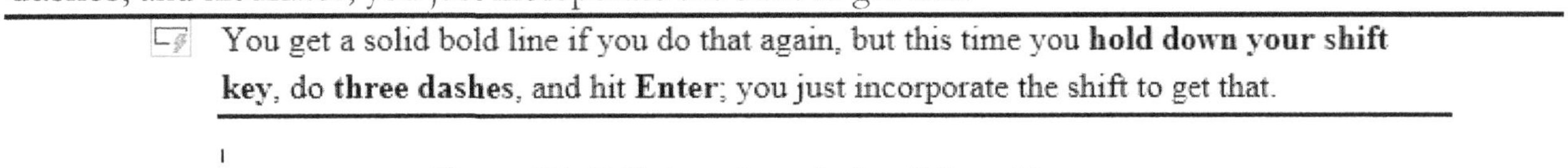

You get a solid bold line if you do that again, but this time you **hold down your shift key**, do **three dashes**, and hit **Enter**; you just incorporate the shift to get that.

Figure 174: Shift then three dashes followed by enter

If you **press Enter** after **pressing Shift** and **three asterisks**, you'll get a dotted line, and if you press Enter after pressing Shift and three-pound symbols, you'll get a different style line.

style line.

Figure 175: Shift then three asterisks followed by enter

Many lie around in autocorrect that you might not be aware of, and they can be quite helpful if you need to get something done quickly. These are excellent illustrations of how Word's autocorrect is implemented and operates.

This Word feature also autocorrects common text shortcuts to their proper characters. So, for example, if you type -->, it automatically corrects to →, (R) changes to ®, the properly registered symbol, and so many others in the list.

But what happens if you want the word that Word has autocorrected? You can undo the autocorrect.

To undo an AutoCorrect:

- Quickly press **Ctrl + Z** or undo before typing any other characters, and if you did not catch it fast,

- Move your cursor to the blue rectangle at the bottom of the first letter of any autocorrect word and click. A menu box appears to undo the autocorrect or do other further settings.

You can edit the Word autocorrect feature, add your own always misspelled word, or remove some words from autocorrecting.

To adjust AutoCorrect Settings:

1. Click the **File** tab to go to the **Backstage**.
2. Select **Options** in the left side menu bar. The **word Option** window appears.
3. Choose **Proofing** in the left side menu.

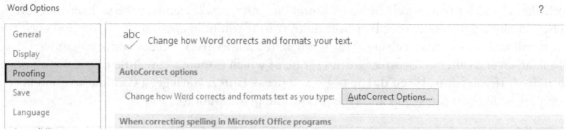

Figure 176: Autocorrect on proofing options

4. Click on the **AutoCorrect Options** button. An autoCorrect dialog box appears with the autocorrect tab active. Click on other tabs as desired. You will see the list of all problems Word fixes for you from the dialog box.

5. Select and press the **Delete** button to remove anyone you do not want word to autocorrect.

6. Add a new entry using the **Replace** and **With** text boxes.

Figure 177: Adding new entry for autocorrect feature

7. Press the **OK** button and close the dialog box.

Changing AutoCorrect's Preferences

If you want to look at how Autocorrect is set up and what autocorrect choices you have selected, go to the **File** tab in the backstage area and scroll down to **"Options"** at the bottom. Then, in the **"Proofing"** section, you'll see autocorrect options at the top. This is where you save all of the autocorrect options if you select **"Autocorrect Options."**

At the top, you have a few options to choose from; by default, they're all selected. In addition, you can **"correct to initial capitals,"** **"capitalize the first letter of sentences,"** the first letter of table cells, the names of the day, and so on by using the autocorrect settings button.

These are all checked, indicating that you want Word to do that. So, for example, if you type the word "Monday" and don't type a capital, you want it to change to a capital. These are some of the most fundamental choices, and you might want to have all of them.

Correcting Your Spelling Errors

Computer software such as Word processing has been an excellent tool for simplifying human needs. However, while trying to construct words, typographical errors can occur, which led Microsoft corporation to look for a means to reduce the possibility of typographical errors while typing. Word has several tools to help you proofread your document and correct any mistakes. However, many don't know how helpful Word 365 is regarding autocorrect and spelling checking. To understand how to autocorrect or scan your document against typographical errors, follow this step-by-step procedure below:

- Make sure you are currently on your document to be corrected

- Go to the "Review" tab

- On your left-hand side, look for "Spelling & Grammar" and click on it

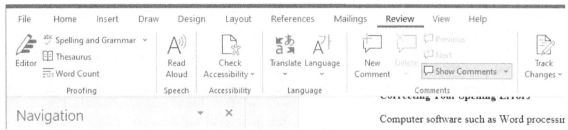

Figure 178: Spelling and Grammar

A dialog box will appear on your right-hand side, starting a spelling check from the first error to the last. For example, the first typographical error could be "Resources" instead of "Resources," so if it was intentionally typed, you click on the "Ignore" option. If not, select the corrected word in the suggestion box, then click on the "Change" option to continue to autocorrect other words.

- Once you select the right suggested words, click on the "Change" option, which will take you to the next misspelled text. Note that if the dictionary feature is installed on your Word 365 and it is a similar word in the dictionary, it will be explained below. If not, click on the "Get a Dictionary" option.

- It is important to note that the spell-checker is not perfect. Sometimes it will say a word is spelled wrong when it is not, such as people's names, street names, and other unique proper nouns. If that happens, you have a couple of different options;

  o The *"Ignore"* option will skip the word one time without changing it.

  o The *"Ignore All"* option will skip the word every time it appears in your document.

  o While the *"Add"* option will permanently add the word to your inbuilt dictionary, so it never becomes an error again. Make sure the word is spelled correctly before using any of these options.

Correcting misspellings one at a time

- Word is designed to mark spelling and grammar errors while you type. That is what the little red and blue wavy lines, as seen in the illustration, are for. Then, you can check your document manually, refer to the marks, and make corrections.

- Red means that there is a spelling error. To correct it, all you have to do is right-click, then choose the proper spelling from the menu, after which the red curly line will be erased.

- Blue means that there is a kind of grammatical error. In this example, it looks like I used the wrong word in the context of the sentence. For example, using *"their"* instead of "there."

Customizing Spelling & Grammar Check

"Word" can be pretty good at picking up on errors like this, but there are certain things that it is set to ignore by default, including sentence fragments, poor sentence structure, and other common grammar mistakes. You must adjust the default proofing settings to include these in your grammar check. To do this,

- Go to the "Backstage view," accessed through your "File menu."

- Click on "Options" on the left pane

- Then, navigate to "Proofing" in the dialog box

- To customize your grammar settings, look for "Writing Style" near the bottom of the Window. Then click the "settings" option located on the right side

- And another dialog box will appear; here, you can set it to check Grammar Only or Grammar & Style, which will cause Word to be strict about the style of your preferred choice. You can also turn specific items on or off to better suit your needs. For example, if you want Word to check for sentence fragments and run-ons, you can turn them on. Ensure you click the "Ok" button once you are through with the changes.

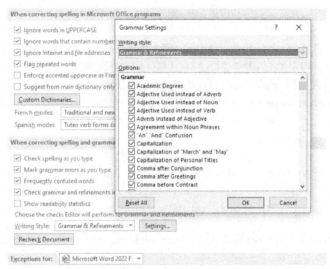

Figure 179: Customizing Spelling & Grammar Check

Finding the Right Word with the Thesaurus

Before I explain "Thesaurus," it is essential to know what "Thesaurus" is. Thesaurus is a tool specially designed into Word by Microsoft to get the synonyms of whatever you are looking for by giving suggestions. So, for example, you can look for "benefit," and you will be given multiple suggestions of synonyms for "benefit," such as "advantage" and "profit," with a classification of which part of speech such words fall under.

Figure 180: Use of Thesaurus

Now, how do we make use of Thesaurus? Simply follow these steps:

- Go to your "Review" tab."

Under the "Review" tab, on your left-hand side, locate "Thesaurus" and double-click on it

- A dialog box will appear on your right-hand side opposite your Navigation pane dialog box, which is located on your left-hand side if activated

- Then, you can type your word or phrase into the "Search" bar. For example, we can look for "Environment" on our "Thesaurus pane" and see what our result will be. You can also type another word of your choice and also see what your result will be

Thesaurus helps you find a word that is similar to your chosen word. Then, it suggests different ways of saying what you want to say.

Making use of the Navigation Pane

For simplicity and flexibility, it is essential to note that you can have your search bar pane through the navigation pane side by side while typing in a Word environment. Follow these step-by-step procedures to achieve that:

- Go to the "View" tab

- Under the "View" tab, on your left-hand side, look for "Navigation Pane," and make sure it is ticked. If not, do so to see the effect on your document.

Figure 181: Navigation pane

- Here is the result; the below "Navigation" dialog box will automatically appear permanently on the left-hand side of your document, except if you untick it from the "View" tab. It enables you to see your listed "Headings," slide "Pages," and search "Result" instantly.

Choosing Language Option

- Go to the "File menu."

- At the displayed interface, click on "Options."

- A dialog box will appear on your left-hand side. Select "Language"

- Then, "Language" features will also appear on your right-hand side. You can choose from the available languages by scrolling through to see other options.

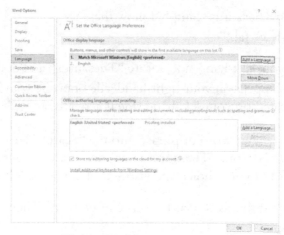

Figure 182: Language settings

- Once done, press the "Ok" option

- Then, you will be instructed to restart Office so your language changes can take effect.

- Take note of your Word 365 interface before restarting your PC. It's by default in the English language

Preventing Text from Being Spell Checked

Certain words in your documents cannot be spell-checked, especially words like address lists, lines of computer codes, and foreign languages such as French, Spanish, etc. To prevent text of this kind from being spell-checked, follow the steps below

- Select the text.

- On the **Review tab**, click the **Language** button, and select **Set Proofing Language.**

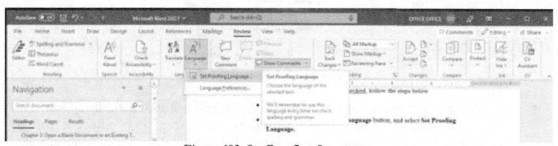

Figure 183: Set Proofing Language

- In the **Language** dialog box**,** click on the **Do not check spelling or grammar** check box

Figure 184: Prevent Text from Being Spell Checked

Here is another approach

- To do this, go to the "Backstage view," which can be accessed through your "File menu."

- Click on "Options" on the left pane

- Then, navigate to "Proofing" in the dialog box

- There are still lots of other ways that you can use to customize your settings depending on your preference. For instance, you can stop Word from marking spelling and grammar errors while you type.

- You can also turn off frequently confused words, like "*there* vs. *their.*" Remember that your spelling and grammar choices apply only to your Word copy. So, if you ignore any error or add a word to your dictionary (for example, your name), those wavy lines will reappear when you send the document to someone else. You can avoid this issue by hiding this document's spelling and grammar errors. Just check the two boxes near the bottom of the Window. When you are done, click "Ok"; now, the errors are hidden.

Hiding Spellings and Grammar Errors in a Document

Suppose you want to share your document with someone and do not want the person to see the red and blue lines. All you need to do is turn off the automatic spelling and grammar checks. Not only will the errors be hidden on your computer, but they also will not be displayed when viewed on another computer. To hide the spelling and grammar errors, follow the steps given below

- Go to the **Backstage view** by clicking on the **File** menu

- Click on **Options** on the left pane

- In the **Word Options** dialog box, click on **Proofing**

- Go to **Exceptions** and click on the checkboxes; **Hide spelling errors in this document only** and **Hide grammar in this document only**

Use of external tools such as Grammarly Plugin

Grammarly is an online tool developed for both web and Word, which has a free and paid version. The free version provides basic word checking, proofreading, and grammar checker, but the upgraded version costs $12.00 per month for one user. In addition, it provides more advanced editing features and allows you to check publications created by your team members in real-time.

Grammarly helps with checking and correcting grammar and spelling errors. Grammarly helps by using specialized software to check the accuracy of your written work, otherwise known as grammar. Grammarly works by detecting the errors that occur when you write sentences in a word processor. It identifies the errors and suggests corrections and fixes that can be made to rectify them. Grammarly also checks your work for plagiarism and smart punctuation. It is capable of detecting more than 250 types of grammatical, spelling, and punctuation mistakes, including improper quotation marks, apostrophes, semicolons, commas, and colon usage. Once you check your work remotely, Grammarly will notify you of grammatical or spelling errors and integrate them with your grammar style guide. It allows users to carry out various functions, such as checking for every single error, then you can learn how to correct the error. The points that help you with this are listed below.

- Grammarly has a free version that helps correct your document's grammar. The plugin is available for Microsoft Word so that it can be installed manually.

- Grammarly also integrates with Microsoft Outlook and provides enhanced grammar checking in emails. You can use this plugin with all email accounts supporting the feature.

- After you have installed this plugin, you will find a Grammarly icon on the menu bar. Click on it and select 'Check grammar, spelling, and style' from the main menu. The process is pretty simple and will take you to a page where you will be guided through the process.

- Once you have created a new document, Grammarly will check that document's spelling, grammar, and style on completion. If it finds any errors, it will highlight them for you to correct.

19 PRINT AND EXPORT

Page Setup

When you initially start a document, it comes with only the default pages, which are all portraits. The first thing you should look at is your **margins**. You may be okay with them by default, but some individuals like to adjust them just to vary the look of their work or to fit more content on their page. You'll be able to fit more content on the page if the margins are smaller.

Setting Up your Margins

You have two rulers in your document: one at the top and the other on the side. If you can't see your rulers, click up to **View** and check **Ruler**. You'll be able to view your margin line after that. Remember that **your margin is the gray area**, while **your document is the white area** where your words will appear. If you want to adjust them, go up to your ruler, and place your mouse between the gray and white sections until it changes into a **double-headed arrow**, click, and you'll see a faint line come up a vertical line, and all you have to do now is pull your margin to the right. As you can see, this has reduced your margin and increased the amount of text on your page. You can repeat the process on the left. These arrows can get in the way, so sometimes you just have to move them out of the way; this will shift part of your text, but don't worry, just grab the margin, in the same manner we did the other side, make sure your cursor is a double-headed arrow, and drag it over to the left once more. Because your arrows up here have moved, you may notice that some paragraphs have been indented. All you must do now is move those back, and everything will fall into place. The left-hand half of this method is a little tricky. Moving your margins up and down to the top and bottom of your page, on the other hand, is significantly easier; you click and drag to shift those margins up or down, and you can do the same with the bottom. By decreasing your margins, you can fit more text on your website. If none of it appeals to you, click the Layout tab and **"Margins."** Then, when you click the drop-down menu, you'll find various options. If you merely want to decrease the size of your margins, **"Narrow"** is an excellent option, and if you click on it, it will automatically modify your margins.

Creating Your Margins

If you wish to choose your margins, navigate to **"Custom Margins."**

A dialog box will emerge when you click that, allowing you to modify the top, bottom, left, and right margins. So, you can use the up or down arrows, and as you do, a tiny little preview will appear here, showing you precisely what you're doing.

Figure 185: Custom margins

Alternatively, you can insert a figure for each of these and click "**OK**" to see how the margins have changed. Once you're satisfied with all of your margins, you can go on to your headers and footers. When you finish a document in Word, you often need to share it. Maybe you're sending it to your boss. Or perhaps you're sharing it with a friend. The way you share your document can change how it looks and works. That's where export options come in.

Different Formats for Different Needs

Word has many formats. Each format has a special use. Think of formats like different types of shoes. You wear sneakers to run and boots in the snow. In the same way, you use different formats for different tasks.

PDF: The Popular Choice

The PDF format is like the sneakers of formats. It's popular and useful. Many people use PDFs because they look the same on all devices. If you send a PDF to someone, it will look the same to them as it does to you. This is great for things like reports or flyers.

DOCX: The Word Standard

DOCX is the standard format for Word. It's like your everyday shoes. If you're sharing a document with someone who has Word, use DOCX. They can edit and change the document if they need to.

RTF: The Safe Bet

RTF stands for Rich Text Format. Think of RTF as the old, reliable boots. It's an older format, but it's safe. Almost all word processors can open RTF. If you're not sure what software someone is using, RTF is a good choice.

Plain Text: Simple and Clean

Plain Text is like sandals. It's simple and doesn't have a lot of extras. It's just text, no pictures or fancy fonts. Use Plain Text when you only need words.

Web Page: For the Internet

If you're putting your document on a website, use the Web Page format. It turns your document into a web page. It's like wearing shoes made for the beach when you're going to the beach.

Other Formats

Word has other formats too. There's ODT for OpenOffice users. There's XML for data tasks. And there are even more. Each format has a job. It's like having hiking boots, dance shoes, and slippers. You use each one for a different thing.

How to Export in Word

Exporting in Word is easy. First, click on 'File' in the top left corner. Then, choose 'Save As'. Pick where you want to save your document. Then, look for the 'Save as type' option. This is where you pick your format. Choose the one you want, and click 'Save'.

How to Print Document

After creating your document by filling it with contents, you may like to print it out to have a feel or send it to someone. Whichever the reason is okay as what is more important is to know how to print your document from your PC. So the first step is to connect the printer to your computer using a suitable cable.

Click on the *File* tab of your document and then the *Print* command. The next step you are to take is to click on the *Print* button again.

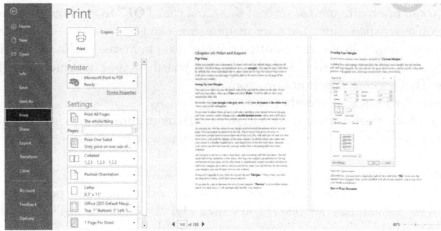

Figure 186: Print a document

Steps in printing Word document

If you want to print more than one document copy, just set it up in that print interface. Also, if you're going to change some settings, do that on that print interface before hitting the last print button. The document will start printing from your printer as soon as you do that. Alternatively, you can open the print interface by using a shortcut.

The shortcut you are to use is pressing the **Ctrl** and the **P** keys on your computer keyboard. This will bring up the print interface. You can then follow the prompts to complete the printing by clicking on the ***Print*** button.

How to Convert Word Document to PDF File

Although a Word document is created and saved in doc or Docx format, you can still save it in PDF format. Also, if you create a document and then decide to send it to someone, the recipient may request you send it in PDF format, so if you learn how to convert that document to PDF format, it will be a plus. There are reasons people prefer to convert their Word documents to PDF. One of the reasons is that PDF files cannot be altered easily compared to Word. But on the other hand, PDF files are usually read-only. So it cannot be edited easily. It is like locking a file for a particular purpose.

To convert your document to PDF, the first step you are to take is to click on the ***File*** tab. When you do this, you will see some options. From those options, click on the ***Export*** command.

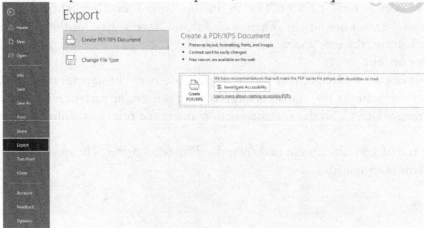

Figure 187: The Export command indicated

As you click on the ***Export*** command, click on the ***Create PDF/XPS*** button.

In the next Window, enter the name you want the document to be identified with. And lastly, click on the **Publish** button. You are done with the conversation once you do that.

Water Marks

A watermark is an image or text that appears behind the document's main text. It is always lighter than the text so you can read the document easily.

a. How to Add Watermark

- Click on the Design tab, and on the right side, you will see an option on the page design known as Watermark.
- Click on the drop-down menu, and you will see some options (Confidential, diagonal, confidential vertical, etc.)
- Click on anyone, and it shows on your document page

b. To Edit a watermark

- On the watermark options, click on the Custom Watermark, and a dialogue box shows up with different options (no watermark, picture watermark, text watermark)
- If you click on the text watermark, click the text you want, the font, the color, layout, and size, and then click on apply. An example of a customized watermark is shown in figure 9 below
- Then the text you typed is applied based on what you filled in the dialogue box.
- To add a picture watermark, select a picture from any folder on your pc, click on Insert, and then click on apply. The picture is shown on your document.

c. How to remove a Watermark

- Click on Design
- Go to watermark and click on Remove Watermark

20 TRACK CHANGES

Tracking Changes to Documents

The Track Changes command allows you to make changes that can easily be spotted or identified. These changes can be reviewed, removed, or made permanent. Changes made in a document are recorded in different colors, with one color for each reviewer, new text is underlined, and deleted text is crossed out.

Turning Track Changes On and Off

To turn on the track changes, follow the steps below

- Go to the **Review tab** and click on **Track Changes** to turn it on. When turned on, the Track Changes button will appear darker than the rest ribbons.

Figure 188: Track changes

- To turn off the **Track Changes**, click on the button again. When the Track Changes is off, Word stops marking changes, but the colored underlines and strikethrough from the changes remain in the documents until they are accepted or rejected.

How to Show and Hide Track Changes

The Display for Review and Show Markup menus control how comments and edits appear

The Display for Review Menu

The Display for Review menu chooses how edits and comments are to be displayed in the document, To locate the **Display for Review** menu, go to the **Review** tab and click on **Display for Review.**

Figure 189: Display for Review

To see how edits and comments are displayed, click on the **Display for Review** drop-down menu, and the options are

- **Simple Markup**: This option displays the changes made on the document with a vertical line in the left margin as an indication.

- **All Markup**: This displays all edits and comments made in the document. New text is underlined, and deleted text is crossed out.

- **No Markup:** This displays the edited version of the document without showing any trace of visible edits or comments.

- **Original:** This displays the document's original version without edits or comments.

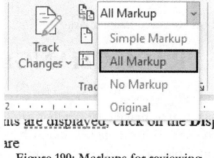

Figure 190: Markups for reviewing

The Show Markup Menu

The **Show Markup** menu allows you to choose the features the Track Changes display
 To locate the **Show Markup** menu, go to the **Review** tab and click on **Show Markup**
To display all comments and edits in your document, select **Show Only Comments and Formatting in Balloons**

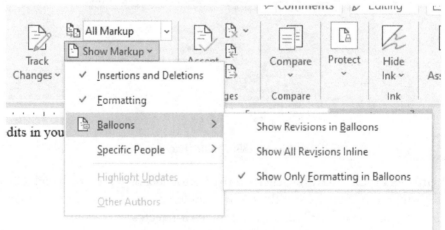

Figure 191: Markup and balloons

Deleting Text with Track Changes

To delete a text with Track Changes, follow the steps below

- Select the text you wish to delete

- Select the **Delete** key on the keyboard. The deleted text will appear with a strikethrough in the All Markup view.

Inserting Text with Track Changes

To insert text with Track Changes, follow the steps below

- Place the cursor where you wish to insert the new text

- Type the new text, and the new text will appear with an underline

Replacing Text with Track Changes

To replace text with track changes, follow the steps below

- Select the text you wish to replace

- Type the replacement text, and the original text will appear with a strikethrough. At the same time, the replacement text will appear with an underline in the All Markup view.

Changing Formatting with Track Changes

Formatting your document involves applying font style, font size, color, italics, etc.

To format text, follow the steps below

- Select the text you wish to format

- Change the format, and the Track Changes will automatically show the selected formatting applied in the document

Accept or Reject Track Changes

Changes made with Track Changes must be accepted before they become part of the document. You can either accept or reject edits individually or all at once.

To accept or reject track changes, select the change made, go to the **Review** tab, and do any of the following

- **Accept a change**: Click the **Accept** button, open the drop-down list on the Accept button, and select **Accept This Change** or **Accept and Move to Next.**

- **Reject a change:** Click the **Reject** button or open the drop-down list on the **Reject** button and select **Reject Change** or **Reject and Move to Next.**

- **Accept all changes:** Open the drop-down list on the **Accep**t button and select **Accept All Changes.**

- **Reject all changes**: Open the drop-down list on the **Reject** button and select **Reject All Changes.**

21 COLLABORATIVE TOOLS

Working together is powerful. Microsoft Word knows this. That's why it has tools to help people work together. These tools are called collaborative tools. They let many people work on one document at the same time. Let's learn about these tools.

21.1 Sharing and Co-Authoring

Sharing is caring. In Word, sharing means letting others see your document. You can let them just look, or you can let them make changes. This is great for team projects. To share a document, go to 'File'. Then, click on 'Share'. You can pick who to share with. You can also pick what they can do. Can they edit? Or can they only view? You decide. When many people work on a document, it's called co-authoring. It's like a team sport. Everyone plays their part. In Word, everyone can type at the same time. You can see where others are typing. Their name shows up. This way, you don't type over each other. Co-authoring is useful. Think about a group report. Everyone can add their part. They can also check each other's work. It's fast and easy. But there's a trick. Everyone needs to use Word online or Word 2016 (or newer). Older versions don't have co-authoring.

Sharing Your Work

Want others to see or edit your document in Word? Here's how:

1. Open your document and look at the top. You'll see the word 'Share'. Click on it.

Figure 192: The Share button

2. Another way is to click on 'File'. Then, choose 'Share' from the options.

Figure 193: Alternative share option

3. If your document isn't saved on OneDrive yet, Word will ask you to do that first. Why? Because OneDrive lets many people access the same file.

4. Now, decide who gets to see your document. There's a drop-down list. Pick from it. Or, type in a name or email.

5. Want to add a note for them? You can! Type your message in the box.

6. Once you're ready, click on 'Send'. Your document is now shared!

Working on a Document Together

Once your document is shared, the fun begins! Everyone can work on it at once.

1. For a smooth experience, use Word's online version. Here, you'll see changes as they happen.

2. Look under 'Share'. You'll see names. These are the people working on the document with you.

3. Notice different colors? These are flags. Each person gets a color. This way, you know who is doing what.

Keeping Track of Edits

Want to see what changes are made? Word has a tool for that as described in Chapter 20 above.

1. Click on 'Review' at the top.

2. Then, choose 'Track Changes'. Now, Word will note all edits.

3. To see these edits, move your cursor to the start of a change.

4. You have choices. Click 'Accept' if you like the change. If not, click 'Reject'. The change will go away.

Real-Time Co-authoring

Got a Word document link in your email? That's an invite to collaborate! Clicking the link will open the document right in your web browser using Word for the web. To start editing, click on 'Edit Document', then choose 'Edit in Browser'. Here's the cool part: If others are editing the same document, you can see them in action. Their edits will pop up live. This magic is what we call coauthoring or live team editing. Want to switch things up? If you prefer using your Word software on your computer, there's an option for that. Look near the top of your screen and switch from 'Editing' to 'Open in Desktop App'. The live team editing feature is available if you have a Microsoft 365 subscription and are using:

- Word 2016 or newer for Windows
- Word 2016 or newer for Mac
- Word on a mobile device (like Android, iOS, or Windows)

But what if you have an older Word version or don't have a subscription? No worries! You can still edit the document while others do. But, you won't see changes as they happen. To view updates from others and share your edits, remember to save the document now and then.

Working with Macro-Enabled Documents (.docm)

Got a document with macros (.docm)? You can still team up and edit! Open and work on the content like any other file, and yes, you can run those macros. If you need to tweak the macro's code, it's easy. Just check out the file, make your changes to the code, and then check it back in.

21.2 Comments and Conflict Resolution

Comments are like sticky notes. You can put them anywhere in a document. They're great for giving feedback. Maybe you like a sentence. Maybe you think something is wrong. Leave a comment!

To add a comment, highlight some text. Then, right-click and choose 'New Comment'. Type what you want to say. Others can see your comment. They can also reply to it. It's like a chat, but in your document. Word's revamped commenting feature enhances team collaboration by introducing features like @mention notifications. This update streamlines the commenting experience across Word and other Office applications, including Excel and PowerPoint. Now, what if two people make different changes? This is a conflict. Word is smart. It will show both changes. Then, the team can decide. Which change is best? Pick one, and move on. Sometimes, conflicts are hard. Maybe two people have strong opinions. It's important to talk. Maybe have a meeting. Remember, the goal is a great document. Everyone should work towards that.

How to View Comments When you insert a comment in Word, it pops up in the right margin, aligning with the relevant text. In this mode, all ongoing comments are displayed in their context. Selecting a comment highlights it and brings it closer to the page.

This view hides all settled comments, allowing you to concentrate on ongoing discussions. To see all comments, including the resolved ones, click on Comments in the toolbar.

Engaging with comments in the Comments section is similar to the main view. If you revisit a settled comment, it reappears in the main view.

Switch between views anytime by selecting Comments on the toolbar's right side.

Adding Comments A noticeable change in the updated comments is the "Post comment" button, which you need to click to finalize the comment.

Alternatively, press Ctrl + Enter (or Cmd + Enter on MacOS) to post. This change ensures you have full control over your comments. Previously, comments were live as you typed, allowing collaborators to view incomplete comments. Now, you can review and adjust your comments before finalizing them.

Commenting on a Document

Commenting on a document is a great way of referring to it later and understanding your reason for particular tagged content.

Entering comments

- Select the content you want to comment on by highlighting it

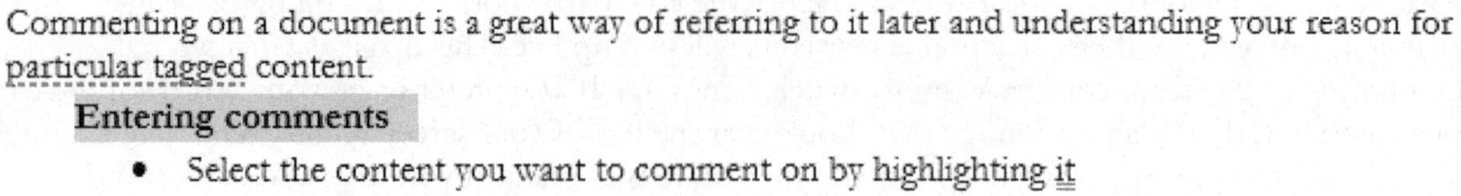

Commenting on a document is a great way of referring to it later and understanding your reason for particular tagged content.

Entering comments

- Select the content you want to comment on by highlighting it

Figure 194: Select content to comment

- Once your text has been selected, simply go to the "Review" tab
- Under the "Review" tab, you will see "New Comment" below it

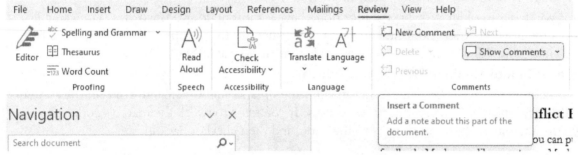

Figure 195: Inserting a comment

- You may also use the shortcut Ctrl + Alt + M.
- Enter "New Comment" by clicking on it, your highlighted text will be colored and another dialog box will appear on your right-hand side, the little "speech bubble rectangular shape" is a symbol or a referrer to your "comments box" at your left-hand side

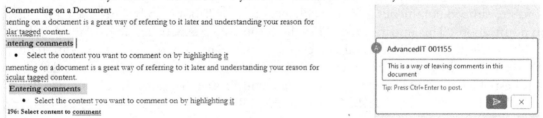

Figure 196: Writing your comment

The functionality of the updated comments remains familiar. You can respond to, modify, erase, or settle a comment thread within the comment itself.

For enterprise users with documents saved online, the @mention feature lets you direct a comment or response to a specific individual.

Replying to comments

- Input your text inside the "Comment box", since our text is centered on "Commenting", I will be typing "Commenting Instruction", note below is another session to also "Reply" on your comment, just like an online post.

Figure 197: Replying to a comment

Note: don't be confused with the name "Unlimited" it is my PC name that I used, yours might not be "Unlimited", what your PC name is stored as is what will reflect on your comment session and your comment duration period after dropping your comment will be noted.

- You can reply on "Comment" with any word assuming I typed "More details on printing procedures" as my "Reply".

Note that on a single comment, your "Reply" does not have limits.

Resolving comments

- Highlight the comment or reply to be resolved or right-click on it to resolve it

Viewing and Displaying Comments

- Go to the "Review" tab
- You will see "Show Comments"
- Or on your document, you will notice a little speech rectangular icon, once you click on it, it will display your comments
- Your comment box will be displayed again for viewing or editing purpose

Fixing Common Coauthoring Issues in Word for Windows

Every so often, while working together in Word, you might bump into an error. Don't worry! Here's a guide to help you out.

Issue: Upload Failed - Save as / Discard

What you see: An error bar pops up, AutoSave stops, and updates halt. Your work is safe on your computer, but you can't collaborate until this is fixed.

Reason: Your document isn't syncing because your changes clash with someone else's.

Solution:

1. If you've made changes you want to keep, click on Save a Copy and save with a new name.
2. Open the shared document again.
3. Re-add any edits that didn't sync.

Issue: Upload Failed - Resolve Conflict

What you see: An error bar pops up, AutoSave stops, and updates halt. Your work is safe on your computer, but you can't collaborate until this is fixed.

Reason: Your changes are conflicting with someone else's. Using AutoSave can help avoid this.

Solution:

1. Click on Resolve.
2. Use the Conflicts tab to go through each change.
3. Accept or reject each one.
4. Close the conflict view when done.

Issue: Recovered Conflicts

What you see: Your document reopens on its own with an error bar. You're connected to the shared document, but any clashing changes are marked as tracked changes by Microsoft Word.

Solution:

1. Click on the Review Changes button in the error bar to see the conflicting edits.
2. For a clearer view, select All Markup, then Show Markup, and pick Microsoft Word.
3. In the Review tab, go through each tracked change made by "Microsoft Word."

Issue: Refresh Recommended

What you see: An error bar pops up, AutoSave stops, and updates halt. Your work is safe on your computer, but you can't collaborate until this is fixed.

Reason: There's a newer version online, and your document can't update on its own.

Solution: Click on Refresh and get back to collaborating.

Issue: Automatic Refresh

What you see: Your document reopens on its own, showing the latest changes.

Solution: Word updated your document for you. Continue working!

Issue: Upload Pending

What you see: A progress bar or an error message might appear.

Reason: Your document isn't syncing, likely due to internet issues.

Solution: Keep Word open with AutoSave on. Word will keep trying to save your work until it can.

Addressing Coauthoring Issues in Word for macOS

From time to time, while collaborating in Word on macOS, you might encounter an error. Here's a guide to help you navigate these issues.

Issue: Upload Failed - Save as / Discard

What you notice: An error bar shows up, AutoSave deactivates, and updates stop. Your work is stored on your computer, but collaboration is paused until the issue is resolved.

Reason: The document isn't syncing to the server due to conflicting edits with others.

Solution:

1. To keep any changes, click on Save a Copy and save with a different name.
2. Open the shared document again.
3. Re-introduce any edits that didn't sync.

Issue: Recovered Conflicts

What you notice: The document reopens automatically with an error bar. You're now linked to the shared document, but conflicting edits are marked by Microsoft Word.

Solution:

1. Click on the Review Changes button in the error bar to see the conflicting edits.
2. For clarity, choose All Markup, then Show Markup, and pick Microsoft Word.
3. In the Review tab, go through each tracked change made by "Microsoft Word."

Issue: Refresh Recommended

What you notice: An error bar shows up, AutoSave deactivates, and updates stop. Your work is stored on your computer, but collaboration is paused until the issue is resolved.

Reason: There's an updated version online, but your document isn't updating automatically.

Solution: Click on Refresh to resume collaborating.

Issue: Automatic Refresh

What you notice: The document reopens automatically, reflecting the most recent changes.

Solution: Word updated your document for you. Dive back into your work!

Task Assignment For those using Word online, comments and @mentions can also be used to delegate tasks. Simply @mention a colleague and check the "Assign to" box to designate the comment as a task.

22 ACCESSIBILITY FEATURES

Microsoft Word, a tool many of us use daily, has been designed with everyone in mind. This includes those who might have different abilities and needs. Let's dive into the accessibility features of Microsoft Word.

Why Accessibility Matters

Accessibility is about making sure everyone can use a product, regardless of their abilities. Think about a ramp at a building entrance. It's there to help people in wheelchairs get inside. But, it also helps someone pushing a stroller or pulling a suitcase. In the same way, Microsoft Word's accessibility features help all users, not just those with disabilities.

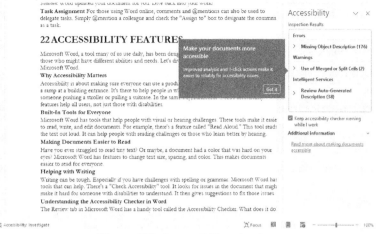

Figure 198: Accessibility checker

Built-In Tools for Everyone

Microsoft Word has tools that help people with visual or hearing challenges. These tools make it easier to read, write, and edit documents. For example, there's a feature called "Read Aloud." This tool reads the text out loud. It can help people with reading challenges or those who learn better by hearing.

Making Documents Easier to Read

Have you ever struggled to read tiny text? Or maybe, a document had a color that was hard on your eyes? Microsoft Word has features to change text size, spacing, and color. This makes documents easier to read for everyone.

Helping with Writing

Writing can be tough. Especially if you have challenges with spelling or grammar. Microsoft Word has tools that can help. There's a "Check Accessibility" tool. It looks for issues in the document that might make it hard for someone with disabilities to understand. It then gives suggestions to fix those issues.

Understanding the Accessibility Checker in Word

The Review tab in Microsoft Word has a handy tool called the Accessibility Checker. What does it do? Well, it's all in the name. When you use the Accessibility Checker, it looks over your document. It then tells you if there are parts that might be hard for people with disabilities to understand. It's like having a helpful friend who gives you advice on how to make your work better for everyone. One common issue it finds is "missing alt text." What's that? Let's say you add a picture to your document. Alt text is a short description of that picture. It helps people who can't see the picture understand what's in it. If you forget to add alt text, the Accessibility Checker will remind you. The Accessibility Checker has more tools to help you out. When you click on it, you'll see a list of options. These options include Alt Text, Navigation Pane, Focus, and more. Each option has a specific job. For example, if you choose Alt Text, Word will show you which pictures or objects in your document need descriptions. Then, you can add the missing alt text. In short, the Accessibility Checker is like a guide. It helps you make sure your document is easy for everyone to read and understand. Whether they can see the pictures or not, everyone gets the full story.

Using Voice Commands

Some people might find it hard to type. Maybe due to a physical challenge or an injury. For them, Microsoft Word has voice commands. You can speak, and Word will type for you. You can even edit and format your document using just your voice.

Navigating with Ease

For those who can't use a mouse, navigating a document can be hard. But, Microsoft Word has keyboard shortcuts. These shortcuts allow users to do everything they'd do with a mouse, but using the keyboard.

Customizing for Your Needs

Everyone is different. What works for one person might not work for another. That's why Microsoft Word lets users customize its features. You can adjust settings to fit your needs. Whether it's changing font size or using a specific tool more often.

Feedback is Key

Microsoft is always looking to improve. They want to make sure their tools work for everyone. If you ever feel like something could be better, you can give feedback. Microsoft listens to users to make their products better.

Inclusion is the Future

In today's world, everyone should have the same opportunities. Tools like Microsoft Word are making sure of that. By offering features that help all users, they're making the world a more inclusive place.

23 SECURITY AND PRIVACY

Microsoft Word is a powerful tool. Many of us use it daily. But how often do we think about its security features? Not much, right? Yet, it's crucial. We store personal and work-related data in our documents. We need to keep them safe.

Protecting Your Privacy in Office

Using Office, you can easily create, display, and share data. But, you can also keep your data private. Here's how:

Edit Personal Information in All Office Documents

Office automatically adds your author and contact details to documents. If you want to change or remove this:

- Open Word and click on File.
- Click on Options then head to General.
- Edit or delete the details as needed.

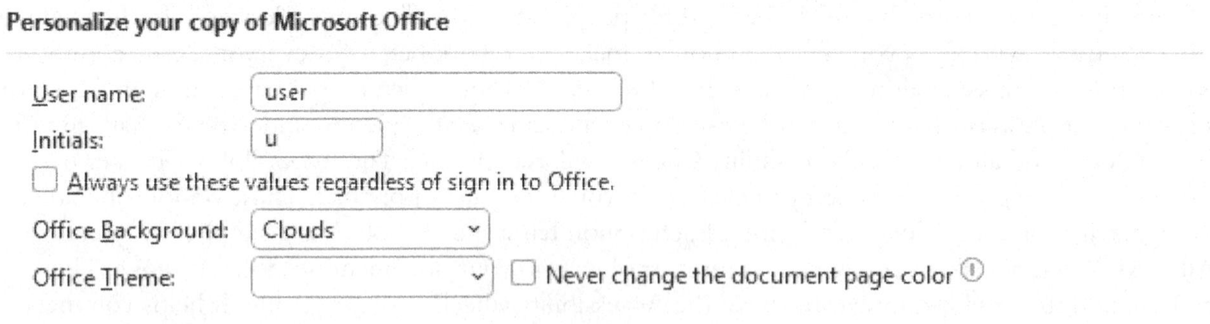

Personalize your copy of Microsoft Office

User name:	user
Initials:	u

☐ Always use these values regardless of sign in to Office.

Office Background: Clouds ⌄

Office Theme: ⌄   ☐ Never change the document page color ⓘ

Figure 199: Username setting

Remember: Changing this in one Office app updates it for all apps.

23.1 Password Protection

One way to protect your document is by adding a password. When you set a password, only those who know it can open the file. It's like locking your house when you leave. It keeps unwanted visitors out.

Setting a password is easy. Go to the File tab. Choose Protect Document. Then, select Encrypt with Password. Type your password. Remember it! If you forget, you can't open the file.

But, be careful. If someone guesses your password, they can access your document. So, choose a strong password. Mix letters, numbers, and symbols. Avoid using easy-to-guess words.

Microsoft Word, a key component of the Office suite, has been evolving since its debut in 1983. With its widespread usage, even by institutions like the Department of Defense, it's no surprise that Word offers a robust password protection feature. This feature, enhanced over the years, now boasts a strong 256-bit encryption, making your documents secure.

However, two crucial points to note:

1. If you forget the password, Word doesn't offer a recovery option. So, a forgotten password means inaccessible content.
2. This password feature is exclusive to the desktop version. Neither the online nor mobile versions support it.

Now, let's walk through the simple steps to secure your Word document with a password:

Securing Your Office Document with a Password

To add a layer of protection to your Microsoft Word, Excel, or PowerPoint files, follow these steps:

1. Launch the desired Office document.
2. Navigate to File menu, located at the top-left corner..
3. Choose Info from the drop down.
4. On the right pane, select Protect document.

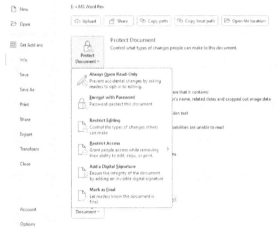

Figure 200: Protecting your Word file

5. Pick the Encrypt with Password option.
6. A prompt will appear. Enter a secure password.

Figure 201: Enter your password

7. Hit the OK button.
8. Confirm the password by entering it again.

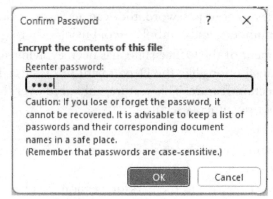

Figure 202: Confirm the password

9. Press the OK button.

After these steps, you'll need to provide the password every time you wish to access the document. Remember, if you lose this password, accessing the document becomes nearly impossible. So, store it safely.

Removing Password Protection from an Office Document

If you decide to remove the password from a Word, Excel, or PowerPoint file, here's how:

1. Open the protected Office document.
2. Input the existing password to unlock it.

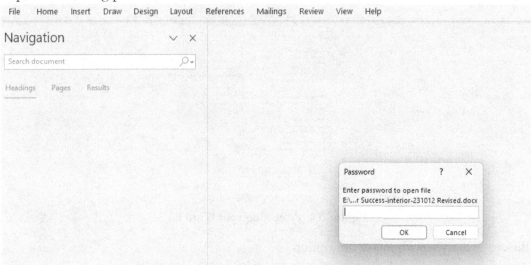

Figure 203: Opening the file requires a password

3. Press OK.
4. Head to File.
5. Choose Info.
6. In the right pane, select Protect document.
7. Opt for Encrypt with Password.
8. Erase the existing password from the field.
9. Click OK.

By following these steps, your document will no longer require a password for access, making it accessible to anyone.

23.2 Permission Management

Another security feature is permission management. This lets you decide who can do what with your document. For example, you can allow someone to read the file but not make changes. To set permissions, go to the File tab. Choose Protect Document. Then, select Restrict Editing. You'll see options. You can decide who can edit and who can't. It's like giving keys to trusted people but keeping the master key for yourself.

Safeguarding Documents with Information Rights Management in Word

Information Rights Management (IRM) is a tool that aids in safeguarding sensitive data from unauthorized access, copying, or sharing. This system stores permissions within the document, which are then authenticated by an IRM server. With Microsoft 365's IRM, you can manage permissions for XML Paper Specification (.xps) files and these Word file formats:

- Regular Documents: .doc, .docx
- Macro-enabled Documents: .docm
- Templates: .dot, .dotx
- Macro-enabled Templates: .dotm

Setting Up Your Computer for IRM

For Microsoft 365's IRM to function, you need at least the Windows Rights Management Services (RMS) Client Service Pack 1 (SP1). The RMS admin can set up specific IRM policies that dictate access and editing levels for an email. For instance, an admin might create a "Company Confidential" rights template. This would mean an email using this policy can only be accessed by users within the company's domain.

Getting Permissions

The first time you access a restricted document, you'll need to connect to a licensing server to confirm your identity and get a use license. This license outlines your access level to a file. This process is mandatory for each restricted file. When obtaining permissions, Microsoft 365 sends your credentials, including your email address and permission rights, to the licensing server. The document's content remains secure and isn't sent.

Limiting Access to File Content

With IRM, you can set restrictions based on individual users, files, or groups (group-based permissions need Active Directory). For instance, Albert might allow James to read a document but not edit it. Meanwhile, Alex might have editing rights. Albert can also set a five-day access limit for both.

To set this up:

1. Open the document.
2. Click on File.
3. Choose Info, then Protect Document.
4. Select Restrict Permission by People, followed by Restricted Access.

Figure 204: Restricted Access

5. In the Permissions dialog, choose the desired access levels for each user.

Access Levels Explained

- **Read**: Users can view but not edit, print, or copy.
- **Change**: Users can read and edit but can't print.
- **Full Control**: Users have complete access, including setting expiration dates and granting permissions.

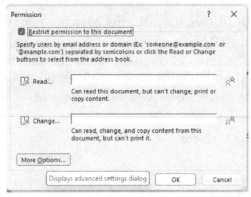

Figure 205: Permission levels

After setting permissions, the author or those with Full Control can always access the document.

Setting an Expiry Date

1. Open your file.
2. Click on File.
3. Under the Info tab, select Protect Document.
4. Choose Restrict Permission by People, then Restricted Access.
5. In the Permissions dialog, select More Options.
6. Choose the expiration date.

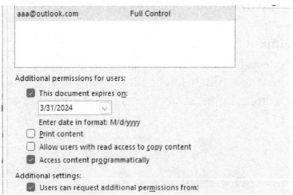

Figure 206: Setting expiry date for restricted access

7. Confirm with OK.

Viewing Restricted Content

To see rights-managed content you have access to in Microsoft 365, simply open the document. If you want to see your permissions, select View Permission in the Message Bar.

Document Inspection

Before sharing a document, it's good to check it. Why? Because it might have hidden data. This data can reveal more than you want. Microsoft Word has a Document Inspector. It finds and removes hidden data.

To use it, go to the File tab. Choose Check for Issues. Then, select Inspect Document. The tool will show you what hidden data is in your file. You can choose to remove it.

Digital Signatures

Have you heard of digital signatures? They're like a seal of approval. They show that a document hasn't been changed since it was signed. It's a way to prove that the file is genuine.

To add a digital signature, go to the File tab. Choose Protect Document. Then, select Add a Digital Signature. You'll need a signature service. If you don't have one, Word can suggest options.

Macro Security

Macros are sets of commands. They make tasks easier in Word. But, they can be risky. Why? Because bad people can use them to harm your computer. Microsoft Word lets you control macros. You can decide which ones to run and which ones to block.

To set macro security, go to the File tab. Choose Options. Then, select Trust Center. Click Trust Center Settings. Choose Macro Settings. You'll see options. Pick the one that suits you best.

Read-Only Documents

Sometimes, you want to share a file but not let others change it. You can make your document read-only. This means people can view it but not edit it.

To do this, go to the File tab. Choose Save As. Pick a location. In the Save As dialog box, click Tools. Choose General Options. Check the Read-only option. Save your document.

Backup Copies

Losing a document is a nightmare. But, accidents happen. What if you could have a backup? A copy that's saved just in case? Microsoft Word lets you do this.

To set up backups, go to the File tab. Choose Options. Click Save. Check the Always create backup copy option. Now, Word will save a backup each time you save your document.

Document Encryption

Encryption is like a secret code. It scrambles your document's data. Only those with the right key can read it. Microsoft Word offers this feature.

To encrypt a document, go to the File tab. Choose Protect Document. Select Encrypt with Password. Enter a password. Your document is now encrypted.

Trusted Locations

Some files are safe. You trust them. Microsoft Word lets you set trusted locations. These are places on your computer where you store trusted files.

To set trusted locations, go to the File tab. Choose Options. Click Trust Center. Choose Trust Center Settings. Click Trusted Locations. Add the places you trust.

Updates and Patches

Software isn't perfect. Sometimes, there are flaws. But, Microsoft works hard to fix them. They release updates and patches. These improve security. It's essential to keep your Word updated.

To check for updates, go to the File tab. Choose Account. Click Update Options. Choose Update Now. Word will check for updates. If there are any, it will install them.

24 THE POWER OF AUTOMATISM

The power of automatism: what's VBA, what's a MACROs, how to register a macro to do repetitive operations quickly, where download Word templates for different needs (articles, CVs, motivational letters, contracts, book, thesis, job offer, etc.)

Understanding the Macros

In Microsoft Word, a macro is like a digital assistant that remembers a set of tasks you teach it. Macros in MS Word are sequences of commands and actions that automate repetitive tasks. Think of them as shortcuts to execute multiple steps with a single command.

Imagine teaching someone how to tie a shoe; once they learn, they can do it again without guidance. Similarly, when you record a macro, you're teaching Word a sequence of steps, which it can then repeat on command. Word Macros are scripts that perform actions, like running formulas or inserting templates. Creating Macros in Word is easy and requires no special skills. To begin, you must assign a key combination to perform the actions. Next, you can create and edit a macro using the VBA editor, accessible by pressing the shortcut key ALT + F11. Macros are small pieces of code written in a programming language. They are not immune to errors or virus threats, so it is essential to use proper code. Incorrect codes will break your macros. Also, macros should not interfere with other Word commands. If you are unsure of a macro, you can search for it in the Macros dialog box. You must enable the macro option in Word to enable macros in Microsoft Word. The macro icon looks like a tape and is blue. Clicking it will record the action you want. Once it is complete, you can then use it to edit your document. The macro icon is located in the View tab. Macros are useful for a variety of tasks. For example, using Find and Replace to replace multiple words can be tedious. Macros make it easier for you to highlight words you use often. Whether searching for multiple synonyms or highlighting multiple words, a macro can be tailored to perform these tasks quickly.

24.1 Why Use Macros?

Macros are all about efficiency. Here's why they're handy:
1. **Uniform Look for Documents**: If you want all your documents to have the same look, instead of manually setting the format each time, just teach Word once using a macro, and then let it do the job for you where the macros can apply a set of predefined formatting rules.
2. **Work with Other Programs**: Macros aren't limited to Word. They can pull data from Excel, fetch information from databases, or even create reports by merging data from various places.
3. **Handle Complex Tasks**: If you're dealing with intricate calculations or data manipulation in Word, macros can be your best friend. Instead of doing the heavy lifting yourself, let the macro handle it.
4. **No More Repetition**: If there's something you do often, like inserting a specific table or applying a particular style, a macro can do it for you in a flash.

Macro Types in MS Word:
1. **Keystroke Macros**: These are straightforward sequences captured by recording a series of actions.
2. **Scripted Macros (VBA)**: These are more advanced and involve writing code using Visual Basic for Applications (VBA). While VBA is versatile, it's not always the best choice for intricate document assembly due to its general-purpose nature.

How to Teach Word a New Macro?
Here's a step-by-step guide:
1. Creating the Macro

You should understand the actions you wish to record before recording your macro.

Activate the Developer Tab: First, make sure you can see the 'Developer' tab on Word's ribbon. If it's hiding, go to Word Options, choose Customize Ribbon, and tick the 'Developer' option.

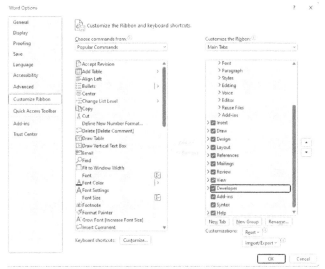

Figure 207: Activating Developer Tab

Click View Tab

Click the Macros options to display a down menu

Choose Record Macro

Figure 208: To record a macro

Alternatively, enable the Developer tab. Then, go to the Code section and click Record Macro.

Figure 209: Using developer tab

A Record Macro dialog box will appear asking for a name. Type in your preferred Macro name. Choose something that describes the task, so you remember its purpose later. Do not use any space. Select the Button option since we will add it to Quick Access Toolbar (QAT).

Shortcut (Optional): If you want a quick way to run your macro, assign it a keyboard shortcut.

    2.   Add Macro to QAT

Go to the Word Options dialog box and heat to Customize the Quick Access Toolbar. Next, choose the created Macro that appears on the left before clicking on Add.

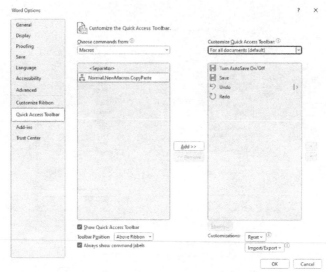

Figure 210: Adding created macro to QAT

You may modify the name if you wish to do so. You can also change the icon for your button.

3. Once you complete, click OK.

Select the position to save your Macro. Decide if this macro should be available only for the current document or for any document you work on in the future. It is stored in the Normal template by default.

4. Set a description for your Macro

In the description box, enter a descriptive term if you so wish.

Click OK, which takes you back to Word Options, where you also click Ok.

5. Record the desired actions

You will realize the cursor has a cassette tape icon. An implication is that it is the macro recording mode. Do the actions you wish to be part of your macro.

6. Stop the recording

Once you are done, click the View tab. Next, click the down arrow on the Macros button and click on Stop recording.

7. Run your macro

Open a new Word document.

Click the Setup button appearing on the Quick Access Toolbar.

To activate a macro, you have a few options:

1. Simply press its designated button on the Quick Access Toolbar as described above.
2. Use its keyboard shortcut.
3. Or, follow these steps:
   - Go to the View tab.
   - Select Macros, then choose View Macros.
   - From the list that appears, pick the macro you wish to activate.
   - Finally, hit the Run button.

Sharing a Macro Across Documents

To ensure a macro is accessible in every new document, you'll need to save it to the Normal.dotm template. Here's how:

1. Open the document containing your macro.
2. Navigate to View > Macros > View Macros.
3. Select Organizer.
4. Highlight the macro you wish to transfer to the Normal.dotm template and hit Copy.

Adding a Macro Button to the Toolbar
1. Go to File > Options > Customize Ribbon.
2. From the "Choose commands from" dropdown, select Macros.
3. Highlight the desired macro.
4. Under "Customize the ribbon," select the tab and the custom group where you'd like the macro to appear.
5. If you haven't created a custom group yet, select New Group. Then, click Rename to give your group a name.
6. Press Add.
7. Click Rename again to select an icon for your macro and provide a suitable name.
8. Confirm your changes by clicking OK twice.

Diving into VBA

VBA (Visual Basic for Applications) is the backbone of macro scripting in MS Word. It's a programming language that extends the capabilities of Word beyond its standard features. However, for document assembly, VBA has its limitations. For instance, it lacks tri-state logic, which is essential for conditions that aren't just true or false but might also be unknown.

Figure 211: The VBA of the CopyPaste macro

Do You Need Programming Skills for Macros?

Not necessarily! While VBA involves coding, many simple macros can be created using Word's built-in macro recorder, which captures your actions and translates them into VBA code.

Recording Macros:

The Developer tab in Word provides tools for macro management. The 'Record Macro' button is especially useful for beginners. It captures your actions in Word and translates them into VBA code, providing a hands-on introduction to VBA programming. However, the generated code can sometimes be hard to decipher, as the recorder makes assumptions based on your actions.

Crafting a Macro in Visual Basic

1. On the Developer tab, within the Code section, choose Macros.
2. In the provided space, enter a name for your macro.
   - Note: If your new macro shares a name with an existing built-in Word macro, your macro will override the built-in one. To see all built-in macros, select Word Commands from the "Macros in" dropdown.
3. In the "Macros in" dropdown, select where you'd like to save the macro. To ensure it's available in all documents, choose Normal.dotm.
4. Click Create, which will launch the Visual Basic Editor.

For those unfamiliar with the Visual Basic Editor and looking for more guidance, you can access the Microsoft Visual Basic Help by selecting Help or pressing F1.

24.2 Inserting Equations in Word Document

Word is built so that people from different areas of discipline can use it. Whether you specialize in Mathematics, Physics, or Chemistry, Microsoft Word has some already designed equations that you can insert in the document you create to communicate the information you need to your students or readers. You do not need to overthink how to create the contents of the equations individually because that has been put together for you by Microsoft in their MS Word document.

To insert an equation or equations in your Word document, click on the **Insert** tab first. This action will then display some commands. The next step you are to take is to click on the dropdown of the **Equation** command. This command is positioned in the right-hand hand corner. It is indicated in the photo below.

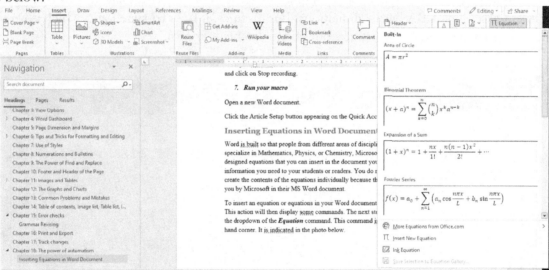

Figure 212: Inserting formulas in Word

As you can see in the above photo, some equations are displayed. You can scroll down until you get to the equation you want to use, click on it, and it will be inserted into your document. In addition, if the equation you want to insert in your document is not found on the list as you scroll down, there are other options to display more equations. For example, as you click on the dropdown of the **Equation** command, take your cursor down and click on *More Equations from Office.com*. When you take this action, more equations will be displayed. You can then click on the one you want to be applied to your document. If the above approach does not give you the equation for the work you want, you can click on **Insert New Equipment** or **Ink Equation**. When you select the former, you will be allowed to type or draw the equation you want by yourself. And if you go with the latter, Word will allow you to insert the Mathematical equation you need in the document through handwriting. Your equations are essential to Microsoft, which is why they provide you with many options to get the job done. When you use the handwriting approach, as you write, it is corrected automatically to what you want. If, for instance, you write a symbol and it is changed to another one, do not be troubled by trying to correct that one that was misinterpreted. Instead, keep writing; at the end, Word will change it to what you want. It is an app that works with the help of artificial intelligence.

Using Symbols in Your Document

Symbols communicate important messages to people. For example, you may be typing on your document and, at a point, needs to insert a symbol or symbols at a spot. To achieve that, you need to know how to do it. To insert a symbol in your Word document, click on the spot of your document where you want it to be placed. Next, click on the **Insert** tab. You will see some commands under this tab. First, drag your cursor to the top-right corner and then click on **Symbol,** which is indicated in the photo below.

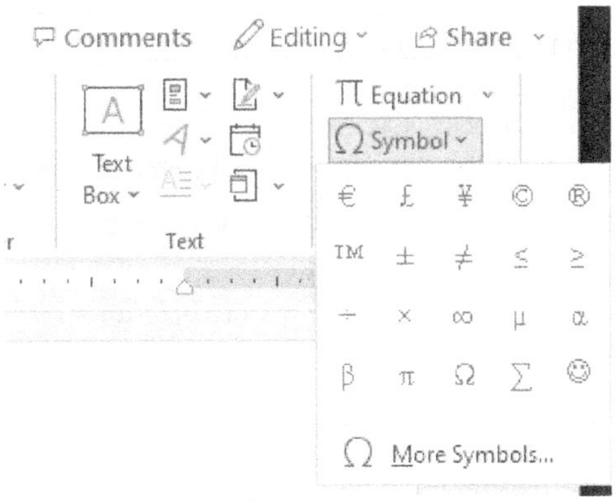

Figure 213: The symbol command

On clicking on the *Symbol* command, some symbols are displayed, which you can see in the above photo. Those displayed are popular symbols, and I use them in most cases. But, if the one you want to insert in your document is not there, click on **More Symbols**. As you take that step, you will see many displayed. Just keep scrolling until you get to the one you want to have in your document. As you get to it, click on it and click on the **Insert** button as well.

This above action will get that symbol inserted in your Word document. The last step you are to take is to close the symbols dialog box by clicking on the "X" of the dialog box.

To insert a such symbol or special character;
1. Position your cursor where you want to insert the symbol.
2. Go to the **Insert** tab in the **Symbols** group.
3. Click on **Symbol**. A dropdown menu appears.
4. Select the desired symbol if found on the list; otherwise, click on **More Symbols** for more available options.
5. Select your desired symbol.
6. Click **Insert**. The symbol will appear in your document.
7. Then Close the **Symbol** window.

For Special characters:
1. Click the **Special Character** tab in the **Symbol** window (follow steps 1-4 above to open it)
2. Click on the desired character and click the **Insert** button.

There are so many symbols that you can use in this feature. You can change the **font** and the **subset** to view them. Also displayed in the dialog box are the Unicode name and the character name of the selected symbol. You can familiarize yourself with the symbols by changing the font and the subset for you to locate anyone when needed quickly.

25 INTEGRATION WITH OTHER MICROSOFT OFFICE APPLICATIONS

25.1 Linking and Embedding Excel Files in Word Documents

1. Linking Excel to Word: Linking allows your Word document to reflect changes made in the Excel file. Here's how to do it:

a. Open your desired Word document.

b. Open the Excel worksheet containing the data you wish to link.

c. Highlight the cells or the entire worksheet in Excel and copy them.

d. In your Word document, position the cursor where you'd like the data to appear.

e. Right-click and choose either 'Link & Use Destination Styles' or 'Link & Keep Source Formatting'.

f. The Excel data will now be pasted into your Word document. If the Excel data changes, the Word document will automatically update.

Note on Linking:
- If the Excel file is moved, the link in the Word document must be re-established.
- If you're sharing the Word file or using it on another computer, the Excel file must accompany it.
- Editing must be done in the Excel worksheet.

2. Embedding an Excel Spreadsheet in Word: Embedding allows you to insert the entire Excel worksheet into your Word document. There are two methods to do this:

a. Embed as an Object:
- In your Word document, navigate to the 'Insert' tab.
- Click on 'Object' > 'Object'.
- In the pop-up dialog box, go to the 'Create from File' tab.
- Click 'Browse' and select the Excel worksheet you want to embed.
- Click 'OK'. The Excel worksheet will now appear in your Word document.

b. Embed as a Table:
- In your Word document, position the cursor where you'd like the table.
- Go to the 'Insert' tab and click on 'Table'.
- Choose 'Excel Spreadsheet'.
- A blank Excel worksheet will appear in your Word document. You can either enter new data or paste data from another spreadsheet.

Benefits of Embedding:
- The embedded Excel worksheet can be edited directly in Word.
- The Word document's size will increase because the data is stored within the document.
- If the original Excel file is updated, the embedded worksheet in Word won't reflect those changes unless you update it manually.

In conclusion, whether you choose to link or embed depends on your needs. Linking is ideal if you want your Word document to always reflect the most recent data from an Excel file. Embedding is suitable if you want to keep a static version of your Excel data within a Word document.

25.2 Using Mail Merge with Access Data in Word

Mail merge is a powerful tool that allows you to integrate your Access data into Word documents, such as form letters. Here's a step-by-step guide to performing a mail merge using Access data:

1. Preparing Your Access Database:
- Open the Access database containing the addresses or data you wish to merge into Word.
- If the Navigation Pane isn't visible, press F11 to display it.
- Identify the table or query with the required data. If the data is spread across multiple tables, create a select query that consolidates the necessary fields. Use this query for the merge.

2. Initiating the Mail Merge:
- Navigate to the 'External Data' tab in Access.
- In the 'Export' group, select 'Word Merge'.
- The 'Microsoft Word Mail Merge Wizard' dialog box will appear.
- Decide if you want to link your data to an existing Word document or start with a new one.
- Click 'OK'.

3. Using the Word Mail Merge Wizard:
- Word will launch, displaying the 'Mailings' tab and the 'Mail Merge' pane.
- Follow the wizard by using the 'Next' and 'Previous' links at the bottom of the pane.

- **Step 3:** Your recipient list is already determined from Access. However, you can refine it by selecting 'Edit recipient list'. This allows you to exclude specific recipients, apply filters, or sort the list.
- **Step 4:** If you're not using an existing document, write your letter. To insert Access data, position your cursor where you want the data, then choose 'Address block', 'Greeting line', or 'More items' from the 'Mail Merge' pane. Ensure the fields align correctly by selecting 'Match Fields'.
- **Step 5:** Preview the merged data using the 'Next (>>)' and 'Previous (<<)' buttons.
- **Step 6:** To finalize, click 'Print' and choose your desired print options.

4. Wrapping Up:
- Save your Word document and close it.

By following these steps, you can efficiently use mail merge to integrate your Access data into Word, streamlining your document creation process.

26 TROUBLESHOOTING AND SUPPORT

26.1 Troubleshooting Damaged Word Documents

Identifying the Issue: Document Damage or Software Problem?

Word documents can become corrupted, preventing them from opening. This could be due to damage to the document itself or its underlying template. Symptoms include:
- Repeated renumbering or redoing page breaks.
- Incorrect formatting.
- Unreadable characters.
- System crashes or error messages when opening the file.
- Other unusual behaviors.

To determine if it's the document or software:
1. Try opening other Word documents. If they work, the issue might be with the problematic document.
2. Check for similar issues in other Microsoft Office programs. If present, the problem might be with the software or OS.
3. If neither is the case, troubleshoot Word, the Office suite, or the OS.

If the Damaged Document Doesn't Open:

Method 1: Open in Draft Mode Without Updating Links
1. Start Word and select Draft view.
2. Disable automatic link updates and close Word.
3. Reopen Word and try opening the damaged document.

Method 2: Insert the Document into a New Document
1. Create a new blank document.
2. Insert the damaged document into the new one.

Method 3: Create a Link to the Damaged Document
1. Create a new document and type "This is a test."
2. Save it as "Rescue link."
3. Create a link to the damaged document and change its source.

Method 4: Use the "Recover Text from Any File" Converter
1. Open Word and choose "Recover Text from Any File" when opening the document.

If the Damaged Document Opens:

Method 1: Copy Everything Except the Last Paragraph to a New Document
1. Create a new document.
2. Open the damaged document.
3. Copy its contents into the new document.

Method 2: Change the Document's Template
1. Determine the template used by the document.
2. If it's the Normal template, rename it. Otherwise, attach the Normal template.
3. Restart Word and open the document.

Method 3: Start Word Using Default Settings
1. Exit Word and start it using the /a switch.
2. Open the document.

Method 4: Change Printer Drivers
1. Switch to a different printer driver.
2. Check if the issue persists.
3. If necessary, revert to the original printer driver.

Method 5: Force Word to Repair the File
1. Open Word and choose "Open and Repair" when opening the document.

Method 6: Convert the Document Format
1. Save the document in a different format, such as RTF.
2. Open and save it back in Word format.

Method 7: Copy Undamaged Parts to a New Document
1. Create a new document.
2. Open the damaged document.
3. Copy undamaged parts to the new document.

Method 8: Switch Document View to Remove Damaged Content
1. Determine the page where damage starts.
2. Switch to Web Layout or Draft view.
3. Delete the damaged content and save.

Method 9: Open with Notepad
1. Locate the damaged document and open it with Notepad.
2. Clean up the text and save it with a new name.
3. Open the cleaned document in Word and reformat as needed.

Remember, always keep backups of important documents to prevent data loss.

26.2 Troubleshooting Microsoft Word Issues

If Microsoft Word or other Office applications aren't functioning properly, follow these steps:

Step 1: Start Word in Safe Mode Safe Mode helps determine if the issue is caused by Word itself or an external factor, like a COM add-in.
1. Close any open Word documents.
2. Press the Windows key + R to open the Run window.
3. Type **winword /safe** (note the space before the /) and press Enter.
4. If Word operates smoothly in Safe Mode, the issue might be with a COM add-in.

To manage COM Add-ins:
1. In Word, go to File > Options > Add-ins.
2. Under "Manage", select "COM Add-ins" and click "Go".
3. Uncheck all the add-ins and click "OK".
4. Close Word and reopen it to see if the problem persists.
5. If Word works fine, re-enable the add-ins one by one to identify the problematic one.

Note: If you find the "Office Compatibility Pack" among the add-ins, consider uninstalling it from your computer via Control Panel > Add/Remove Programs.

Step 2: Repair Your Office Installation If the issue persists even in Safe Mode, try repairing your Office suite.
1. Right-click on the Start menu and select "Apps & Features".
2. Locate and select your Office installation.

3. Click "Modify" and then choose "Quick Repair". This option fixes many issues without taking much time.
4. If "Quick Repair" doesn't resolve the issue, opt for "Online Repair". This will uninstall and then reinstall Office but won't delete your settings or Outlook data.

Remember to always back up your data before making significant changes to your software.

26.3 Seek Assistance from Microsoft Support Services

Microsoft offers a range of support services tailored to provide you with expert solutions. Whether you're facing a minor glitch or a major issue, Microsoft's team of professionals is ready to assist you. Here's how you can access this support:

1. Personalized Solutions: Microsoft's support team is trained to provide answers tailored to your specific problem. This ensures that you get the most relevant and effective solution.

2. Multiple Support Channels: Depending on your preference and the nature of your problem, you can choose from:

- **Phone Support:** Speak directly with a Microsoft support professional to discuss and troubleshoot your issue in real-time.
- **Chat Support:** Engage in a live chat with a representative. This is especially useful for issues that might require step-by-step guidance.
- **E-mail Assistance:** Describe your problem in detail and get a solution delivered to your inbox. This option is great for non-urgent issues where you can wait for a detailed response.

3. Accessing Support:

- **Direct Access:** Navigate to the Microsoft Office Support home page. Scroll to the bottom of the page where you'll find the various support options available.
- **Through Office Programs:** Some Microsoft Office applications have built-in support links. By accessing these, you can be directed to relevant support resources specifically for that program.

Remember, no issue is too big or small for Microsoft Support. Whether you're a beginner seeking guidance or an expert facing a technical challenge, their team is equipped to assist you.

27 THE STRATEGIC SHORTCUTS

Frequently used shortcuts

BUTTONS	DESCRIPTION
Ctrl + A	Highlight all your content
Ctrl + B	Applying bold to selected text
Ctrl + C	Copy content into the Clipboard
Ctrl + D	Font dialog box
Ctrl + E	Centralized text
Ctrl + F	Navigation for searching
Ctrl + G	Go to a page, section, line number
Ctrl + H	To replace a text
Ctrl + I	Applying italic to selected text
Ctrl + J	To justify your text
Ctrl + K	Insert hyperlink to content
Ctrl + L	Align text to the left
Ctrl + M	Move paragraph
Ctrl + N	Create a new document
Ctrl + O	Open a document
Ctrl + P	Print out document

BUTTONS	DESCRIPTION
Ctrl + R	Align text to the right
Ctrl + S	Save document
Ctrl + U	Applying underline to selected text
Ctrl + V	Paste the copied contents from the Clipboard
Ctrl + W	Close current document
Ctrl + X	Cut the selected content
Ctrl + Y	Redo the previous action
Ctrl + Z	Undo the previous action
Ctrl + [	Decrease the font size
Ctrl +]	Increase the font size
Esc	Cancel a command
Ctrl + Alt + S	Split the document Window
Ctrl + Alt + S	Remove the document Window Split

Access Keys for ribbon tabs

BUTTONS	DESCRIPTION
Alt + Q	Move to the "Tell me" or Search field on the Ribbon to search for assistance or Help content
Alt + F	Open the **File page** to use the Backstage view.
Alt + H	Open the **Home tab** to use common formatting commands, paragraph styles, and the Find tool.
Alt + N	Open the **Insert tab** to insert tables, pictures, shapes, headers, and text boxes.
Alt + G	Open the **Design tab** to use themes, colors, and effects, such as page borders.
Alt + P	Open the **Layout tab** to work with page margins, page orientation, indentation, and spacing.
Alt + S	Open the **References tab** to add a table of contents, footnotes, or a table of citations.
Alt + M	Open the **Mailings tab** to manage Mail, Merge tasks, and work with envelopes and labels.
Alt + R	Open the **Review tab** to use Spell Check, set proofing languages, and track and review changes to your document.
Alt + W	Open the **View tab** to choose a document view or mode, such as Read Mode or Outline. You can also set the zoom magnification and manage multiple documents in Windows.
Alt or F10	Select the **active tab** on the ribbon, and activate the access keys
Shift + Tab	Move the focus to commands on the ribbon.
Ctrl + Right arrow	Move between command groupings on the ribbon
Arrow keys	Move among the items on the Ribbon
Spacebar or Enter	Activate the selected button.
Alt + Down arrow key	Open the menu for the selected button
Down arrow key	When a menu or submenu is open, it's to move to the next command
Ctrl + F1	Expand or collapse the ribbon
Shift+F10	Open the context menu

BUTTONS	DESCRIPTION
• Left arrow key	Move to the submenu when the main menu is open or selected

Navigate the document

BUTTONS	DESCRIPTION
Ctrl + Left arrow key	Move the cursor pointer one space at a time to the left
Ctrl + Right arrow key	Move the cursor pointer one space at a time to the right
Ctrl + Up arrow key	Move the cursor pointer up by one paragraph
Ctrl + Down arrow key	Move the cursor pointer down by one Paragraph
End	Move the cursor pointer to the end of the current line
Home	Move the cursor to the beginning of the current Line
Ctrl + Alt+ Page up	Move the cursor pointer to the top
Page down	Move the cursor pointer by scrolling the document down
Ctrl + Page down	Move your cursor pointer to the next page
Ctrl + Page up	Move your cursor to the previous page
Ctrl + End	Move your cursor to the end of the document

28 FREQUENTLY ASKED QUESTIONS

1. **How do I install Microsoft Word in Microsoft 365?**
   - Navigate to the Microsoft 365 portal, sign in, and click on "Install Office" to download and install Word along with other Office apps.
2. **What are the system requirements for running Microsoft Word in Microsoft 365?**
   - Requirements vary based on the platform (Windows, macOS, etc.). Always refer to the official Microsoft website for the most up-to-date system requirements.
3. **How does the subscription model for Microsoft 365 work?**
   - Microsoft 365 operates on a subscription basis. Users pay monthly or annually for access to Office apps, cloud storage, and other features.
4. **Can I use Microsoft Word without an internet connection?**
   - Yes, once installed, Word can be used offline. However, to access cloud-saved documents or collaborate in real-time, an internet connection is required.
5. **How do I create, save, and open documents in Word?**
   - Click on "File", then choose "New" to create, "Save" or "Save As" to save, and "Open" to open existing documents.
6. **Can I recover a lost or unsaved Word document?**
   - Yes, Word has an AutoRecover feature. Navigate to "File" > "Info" > "Manage Document" > "Recover Unsaved Documents".
7. **How do I format text and paragraphs in Word?**
   - Use the "Home" tab for basic formatting options like font, size, alignment, and spacing.
8. **What are styles, and how can they be utilized in Word?**
   - Styles are predefined formatting options. They can be applied to headings, paragraphs, and more for consistent document formatting.

9. **How can I insert and format tables in my Word document?**
   - Go to the "Insert" tab and choose "Table". Once inserted, use the "Table Tools" tab for formatting.
10. **How do I add and manipulate images in Word?**
    - Use the "Insert" tab and select "Pictures". Once added, use the "Picture Tools" tab for editing.
11. **Can I create graphs and charts within Word?**
    - Yes, go to the "Insert" tab and select "Chart".
12. **How do I use headers and footers in my document?**
    - Navigate to the "Insert" tab and choose either "Header" or "Footer".
13. **What are the different view options available in Word?**
    - Word offers multiple views like "Print Layout", "Web Layout", "Reading View", and "Draft". Access them from the "View" tab.
14. **How can I use the Track Changes feature effectively?**
    - Turn on "Track Changes" under the "Review" tab to monitor edits. You can accept or reject changes individually or collectively.
15. **Can I collaborate with others on a Word document in real-time?**
    - Yes, by saving your document to OneDrive or SharePoint and sharing the link, multiple users can edit simultaneously.
16. **How do I ensure my document is accessible to individuals with disabilities?**
    - Use the "Accessibility Checker" under "File" > "Info" > "Check for Issues".
17. **What security features does Word offer for my documents?**
    - Word provides password protection, restricted editing, and the ability to mark a document as "Read Only".
18. **How can I automate repetitive tasks in Word?**
    - Use "Macros" to record and replay a series of actions or commands in Word. Access this feature under the "View" tab.
19. **Can I use macros in Word, and how do I create them?**
    - Yes, you can use macros in Word. To create one, navigate to the "View" tab, select "Macros", then "Record Macro". Follow the prompts, perform your desired actions, and then stop recording.
20. **What are the most useful shortcuts in Word to improve efficiency?**
    - Some popular shortcuts include Ctrl+C (Copy), Ctrl+V (Paste), Ctrl+Z (Undo), Ctrl+S (Save), and Ctrl+F (Find).
21. **How do I use the Find and Replace feature in Word?**
    - Press Ctrl+F to open the "Find" pane. For "Replace", press Ctrl+H, then input the text to find and its replacement.
22. **Can I insert equations and mathematical symbols in Word?**
    - Yes, go to the "Insert" tab and select "Equation" or "Symbol" to add mathematical content.
23. **How do I create a Table of Contents automatically in Word?**
    - Use styles for headings, then navigate to the "References" tab and select "Table of Contents".
24. **How do I apply and modify numbering and bullet points in Word?**
    - Use the "Home" tab and select either the "Bullets" or "Numbering" icon. Right-click on the chosen style for more customization options.
25. **What are the common mistakes to avoid while using Word?**
    - Avoid inconsistent formatting, neglecting to use styles for headings, not regularly saving your work, and overlooking the built-in grammar and spell check.
26. **How do I troubleshoot issues in Word?**

- Start Word in Safe mode, disable add-ins, or use the built-in "Repair" feature in the Office suite.

27. **Can I use Word on different operating systems, and what are the differences?**
    - Yes, Word is available on Windows, macOS, iOS, and Android. While core functionalities remain consistent, there might be slight variations in interface and features across platforms.

28. **How do I use templates in Word, and can I create my own?**
    - Navigate to "File" > "New" to access templates. To create your own, design your document, then save it as a template via "File" > "Save As" > "Word Template".

29. **How do I print and export Word documents?**
    - Go to "File", then select "Print" for printing options or "Export" for various export formats.

30. **How do I adjust page margins and orientations in Word?**
    - Navigate to the "Layout" tab, where you can adjust margins, orientation, and other page setup options.

31. **Can I use Word in different languages?**
    - Yes, Word supports multiple languages. You can change the editing language in "File" > "Options" > "Language".

32. **What are the new features in the latest version of Word in Microsoft 365?**
    - Features vary based on updates. Refer to the official Microsoft website or Word's "What's New" section for the latest features.

33. **How does Word integrate with other Microsoft 365 applications?**
    - Word integrates seamlessly with apps like Excel, PowerPoint, OneDrive, and Teams, allowing for easy data sharing, collaboration, and cloud storage.

34. **Can I customize the Word interface to my preferences?**
    - Yes, under "File" > "Options", you can customize the Ribbon, Quick Access Toolbar, and other interface elements.

35. **How do I add and edit hyperlinks in Word?**
    - Right-click the text or image and select "Hyperlink". To edit, right-click the hyperlink and choose "Edit Hyperlink".

36. **What are the different break options in Word, and when should I use them?**
    - Under the "Layout" tab, you'll find options like Page Break, Column Break, and Text Wrapping Break. Use them to control content flow and layout.

37. **How can I check and correct grammar and spelling in Word?**
    - Word automatically underlines misspellings and grammar issues. Right-click on the underlined word for suggestions. You can also use "Review" > "Spelling & Grammar".

38. **How do I add captions and references to images and tables in Word?**
    - Right-click on an image or table and select "Insert Caption". For references, use the "References" tab.

39. **Can I protect my Word document with a password?**
    - Yes, go to "File" > "Protect Document" > "Encrypt with Password".

40. **Where can I find additional help and resources for using Word effectively?**
    - Microsoft's official website offers extensive resources, tutorials, and forums. Additionally, the "Help" feature in Word provides guidance on various topics.

29 ENHANCING WORD WITH CHATGPT

Microsoft Word has long been a trusty tool for those who work with words. And now, it has a new friend: ChatGPT.

ChatGPT is like a new kind of magic for Microsoft Word. It's a smart helper that can do many things to make writing easier. Think of it as a friend who's always there to help with your writing tasks. It's not just any friend, though. This friend is super smart and learns more every day.

Now, imagine you are writing a report. You get stuck with grammar or can't find the right word. ChatGPT comes to the rescue! It helps you fix mistakes and find words that fit just right. And it does all of this within Microsoft Word, a place where many of us spend time typing away.

One of the best things about ChatGPT is how it understands what you mean. It can guess what you want to say next. This means it can help you write faster and better. It's great when you need to write something important, like a letter or a project for work.

But why add ChatGPT to Microsoft Word? Well, it's all about making your job easier. It saves you time. It helps you write more clearly. And it even makes sure you don't make mistakes. This means you can write confidently, knowing your work will look professional.

For those who use Microsoft Word a lot, ChatGPT is a game-changer. It brings the power of AI right to your fingertips. You don't have to leave Word to get help with writing anymore. It's all right there, in the same place where you type.

29.1 Overview of ChatGPT

When we think about word processing, the image of a quiet office with the clicking of keyboards comes to mind. But there's a new player in town, and its name is ChatGPT. This friendly AI has become a part of the Microsoft Word experience. It's changing the game for folks like Samantha in Austin, Texas, who's got a lot on her plate but still aims to master Word at work.

ChatGPT is like a smart assistant that's always ready to help. It doesn't just check your spelling; it gives you better words to use. It can even translate your document into another language. This means Samantha can write an email in English and send it in Spanish, just like that. She saves time, and her colleagues are impressed. To get this smart helper working in Word, there's a bit to do first. Samantha will need to set up the system. This might sound tricky, but it's not. There are just a few steps to follow, and if things don't go right, there are tips to fix them. Once it's all set up, Samantha's Word will have some new tricks up its sleeve. Imagine writing a report and getting stuck. ChatGPT can suggest new ways to say things. It's like having a thesaurus that knows exactly what you're trying to say. And for Samantha, who wants to be the Microsoft Word expert at the office, this is perfect. She can learn new words and make her reports shine. What's more, ChatGPT can make big documents easy to handle. It can summarize pages of text into just a few lines. This means Samantha can get the gist of a long report without spending hours on it. And when she needs to make sure everything is right, ChatGPT can check facts and sources. It's like having a little detective right there in Word. Samantha can also make ChatGPT sound like her. If she writes in a friendly way, ChatGPT will too. It learns how she writes and helps in the same style. This means her work feels personal and not like a robot did it. Plus, it can offer advice that feels just for her, helping her get better as she works. Then there's the magic of making boring tasks fast and simple. ChatGPT can create templates for reports or emails in no time. It can even handle complex formatting. This is great for Samantha, who can use these shortcuts to save time. And it can remind her about meetings or deadlines right in Word. It's like having a smart planner on her computer.

The Integration of AI in Word Processing

Imagine a tool in Microsoft Word that helps with more than spelling. ChatGPT is that tool. It does grammar checks and offers better word choices. It even makes sure your tone is just right. It is like having a helper who never gets tired.

ChatGPT can also help you write in different languages. This is big for people who work with teams around the world. You write in English, and ChatGPT can change it to Spanish or Japanese. And the other way around too!

For students, ChatGPT is like a tutor that lives in your computer. It helps with homework. If you write something that is not clear, it gives tips to make it better. It can even help you write a whole essay. Just tell it what you need. But ChatGPT is not just for school. It's for anyone who writes at work. It can write emails or reports. It can even make PowerPoint slides better. And it does all this in Word, a program many people already use. Sometimes, writing can be slow. You have to think of the right words. ChatGPT can speed this up. It gives you suggestions so you can keep writing. This can help you finish faster. And your work will still look great.

Why ChatGPT Makes Microsoft Word Even Better

Millions use Microsoft Word to write simple notes and big projects. Word is already great, but ChatGPT makes it even better. Here's how:

It makes writing quicker and smarter. ChatGPT helps you write good text fast. No more long hours spent on research or drafting. It's really handy for emails, reports, and business stuff.

It's smart about what you need (accuracy and relevance). ChatGPT gets the context. It answers based on what you tell it. You can count on it to be right and on point.

It helps you communicate better. ChatGPT can answer emails or messages quickly. This means you can talk to people better and faster. Whether it's with your team, customers, or anyone else.

Requirements for ChatGPT Integration

Integrating ChatGPT into Microsoft Word requires a combination of technical steps, access to the appropriate tools and services, and some basic programming knowledge. Below are the key requirements to successfully set up ChatGPT within Microsoft Word:

Software Requirements

1. **Microsoft Word**: You need a version of Microsoft Word that supports macros and the developer tab. Typically, the latest versions of Office 365 or Microsoft Office will suffice.
2. **Visual Basic for Applications (VBA)**: VBA should be included with your installation of Microsoft Word, as it's the programming environment you'll use to write and execute your macro script.

Access Requirements

3. **OpenAI API Key**: You must have access to OpenAI's GPT-3 API, which requires an account with OpenAI. After registering and setting up billing (if necessary), you'll receive an API key that allows you to make requests to the GPT-3 service.

Technical Requirements

4. **Basic Programming Knowledge**: Understanding how to write or modify VBA scripts is important. The macro script you'll use is a code that communicates with the OpenAI API, so familiarity with programming concepts will help you troubleshoot any issues.
5. **Internet Connection**: Because you'll send requests to the OpenAI API, a stable internet connection is necessary for real-time data exchange.

Security Considerations

6. **API Key Protection**: Your API key is a sensitive piece of information that should be protected. Avoid sharing the script containing your API key with others, and be cautious about where you store or how you use the script.
7. **Rate Limits and Usage Costs**: Be aware of the rate limits and potential costs associated with using the OpenAI API. Charges may apply depending on the volume of requests and the type of model you're using.

User Interface Adjustments

8. **Custom Ribbon and Macro Button**: You need to customize the Microsoft Word ribbon by adding a new tab and a button to trigger the macro. This involves some familiarity with the Word interface and how to customize it.

Data Handling and Formatting

9. **JSON Handling**: The script formats JSON data to send to the API and parses the JSON response. Understanding JSON structure is helpful.
10. **Text Formatting**: You'll likely want to format the text returned by ChatGPT to fit the style and structure of your Word document. This might include setting font types, sizes, and paragraph styles programmatically.

29.2 Setting Up ChatGPT in Microsoft Word Made Simple

Activating the Developer Tab in Word

First, show or activate the Developer tab—it's hidden by default. Head to "File"> "Options"> "Customize Ribbon." Then, tick the box for "Developer." If needed, you can find more detailed steps in Chapter 24 of this book.

Writing the VBA Script

Open Word, either a new document or one you're working on.

Press "Alt+F11" to start up the VBA editor.

Add a new module: "Insert"> "Module."

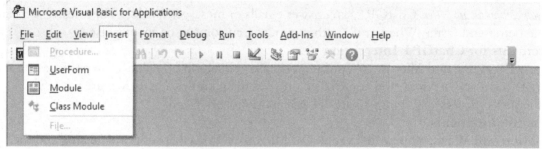

Figure 214: Adding a new module VBA

Copy and insert the provided VBA code below into the new module. Make sure to swap "YOUR_API_KEY" with your actual OpenAI API key.

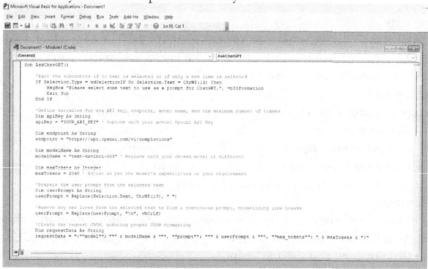

Figure 215: Inserting code in your module

```
Sub AskChatGPT()

    'Exit the subroutine if no text is selected or if only a new line is selected
    If Selection.Type = wdSelectionIP Or Selection.Text = ChrW$(13) Then
        MsgBox "Please select some text to use as a prompt for ChatGPT.", vbInformation
        Exit Sub
```

```
    End If

    'Define variables for the API key, endpoint, model name, and the maximum number of
tokens
    Dim apiKey As String
    apiKey = "YOUR_API_KEY"' Replace with your actual OpenAI API Key

    Dim endpoint As String
    endpoint = "https://api.openai.com/v1/completions"

    Dim modelName As String
    modelName = "text-davinci-003"' Replace with your chosen model if different

    Dim maxTokens As Integer
    maxTokens = 2048' Adjust as per the model's capabilities or your requirement

    'Prepare the user prompt from the selected text
    Dim userPrompt As String
    userPrompt = Replace(Selection.Text, ChrW$(13), " ")

    'Remove any new lines from the selected text to form a continuous prompt, normalizing line
breaks
    userPrompt = Replace(userPrompt, "\n", vbCrLf)

    'Create the request JSON, ensuring proper JSON formatting
    Dim requestData As String
    requestData = "{""model"": """ & modelName & """, ""prompt"": """ & userPrompt &
""", ""max_tokens"": " & maxTokens & "}"

    'Initialize the HTTP request object
    Dim httpRequest As Object
    Set httpRequest = CreateObject("MSXML2.XMLHTTP")

    'Attempt to send the API request
    On Error GoTo ErrorHandler
    With httpRequest
        .Open "POST", endpoint, False
        .SetRequestHeader "Content-type", "application/json"
        .SetRequestHeader "Authorization", "Bearer" & apiKey
        .Send requestData

        'If the request was not successful, show an error message
        If .Status <> 200 Then
            MsgBox "An error occurred: "& .Status &"" & .StatusText, vbExclamation
            Exit Sub
        End If

        'Parse the JSON response to extract the completion text
        Dim responseText As String
        responseText = .responseText
```

```
Dim jsonParser As Object
Set jsonParser = CreateObject("ScriptControl")
jsonParser.Language = "JScript"

Dim completionText As String
completionText = jsonParser.Eval("JSON.parse('""' & responseText &
'""').choices[0].text")

'Insert the completion text into the document after the selected text
With Selection
    .TypeParagraph' Insert a new paragraph
    .TypeText completionText' Insert the completion text
    .TypeParagraph' Insert another new paragraph
    'Optionally format the inserted text
    .Font.Name = "Garamond"
    .Font.Size = 12
    .ParagraphFormat.Alignment = wdAlignParagraphJustify
    .ParagraphFormat.SpaceAfter = 6
End With
End With

'Clean up
ExitPoint:
    Set httpRequest = Nothing
    Exit Sub

ErrorHandler:
    MsgBox "An error has occurred: "& Err.Description, vbCritical
    Resume ExitPoint

End Sub
```

Save your VBA script: "File"> "Save," then close the VBA editor.

Creating the 'AskChatGPT' Button

Go back to Word, then "File"> "Options"> "Customize Ribbon."

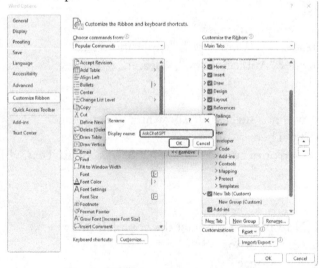

Figure 216: Renaming your new tab

Hit "New Tab," rename it to "AskChatGPT," and do the same for the new group, calling it "Advanced Functions."

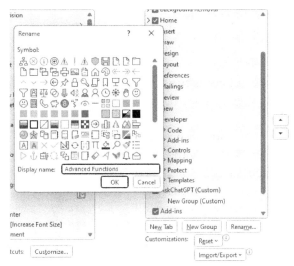

Figure 217: Renaming your group in ChatGPT

Choose "Macros" from the "Choose Commands from" dropdown.
Add your "AskChatGPT" Macro, rename the button to match, pick an icon for it, and hit "OK."

And there you have it, ChatGPT is now at your service within Microsoft Word!

Streamlining Workflow with ChatGPT in Microsoft Word

Having successfully integrated ChatGPT into Microsoft Word, it's time to put this advanced tool to work. To maximize the efficiency and accuracy of ChatGPT in your Word projects, consider the following strategies:

Craft Detailed Prompts: Precision in your prompts is key when working with ChatGPT. Detailed and clear instructions allow the AI to provide responses that closely align with your expectations and requirements.

Explore Various Language Models: ChatGPT comes with various language models, each tailored for different tasks. Trying out various models will help you pinpoint the one that aligns with your specific needs, whether it's for creative writing, technical documentation, or another niche.

Utilize ChatGPT for Brainstorming: ChatGPT excels as a brainstorming partner. Pose a topic or question, and let the AI suggest several ideas. This can significantly speed up the ideation phase of any project.

Revise AI-Generated Content: Remember, the output from ChatGPT is a starting point. To achieve the best results, review and edit the generated text. Fine-tuning ensures that the final output maintains a high standard of quality and suits your document's tone and style.

Leverage ChatGPT Across Applications: While this guide focuses on Microsoft Word, remember that ChatGPT's capabilities can be leveraged across various platforms and applications. This integration can elevate your productivity and assist in multiple aspects of your writing process.

Engaging ChatGPT within Microsoft Word is designed to be a simple, user-friendly experience. Here's a detailed step-by-step guide on how to use ChatGPT to enhance your productivity:

1. Open your Microsoft Word document where you intend to work.
2. Type out the text that you want ChatGPT to process. This could be a question, a statement, or a prompt for content creation.
3. Once you have entered your text, use your mouse or keyboard to highlight the text. Make sure the entire text you want ChatGPT to respond to is selected.
4. Navigate to the 'Advanced Functions' tab at the top of Word. This is a custom tab that you would have previously set up to include the ChatGPT functionality.

5. Within this tab, you will find the 'AskChatGPT' button. Click this button to send your selected text to ChatGPT as a prompt.

6. After a brief moment, ChatGPT's response will be automatically inserted into your Word document directly below the text you had highlighted.

7. To resume the conversation or pose follow-up questions, type a new message, select it, and click the 'AskChatGPT' button again.

Let's take a practical example to illustrate this process:

Imagine you're drafting a Product Specification for a new healthcare technology website requiring an outline to start.

1. In your Word document, type your request for ChatGPT. For example, "Create a detailed product specification outline for a healthcare tech website, focusing on the main features, user interface, and privacy safeguards. Highlight the importance of a smooth patient experience and the capability to integrate with current healthcare infrastructures."

2. Highlight the text you just typed.

3. Click the 'AskChatGPT' button in the 'Advanced Functions' tab.

4. Wait as the AI processes your request and generates a response. This response could be a comprehensive outline, complete with bullet points and subheadings, tailored to the specifications of a healthcare technology website.

5. The response from ChatGPT will be inserted into your document, and you can use it as a foundation to build upon or as a guide for further elaboration.

Troubleshooting Common Setup Issues

"Every problem is a gift—without problems we would not grow." These words ring true, especially when setting up new software. Think of any setup hiccup as a step toward learning something new. In this case, we're tackling common issues you might face when setting up ChatGPT with Microsoft Word.

First off, some people might see an error message during installation. This often means your computer or Word isn't up to date. So, check for any updates and install them. Updates are like fresh starts—they can clear up a lot of problems.

Then there's the hiccup where ChatGPT doesn't appear in Word after installation. If that happens, don't fret. Sometimes, all it takes is restarting Word. If that doesn't work, try a computer reboot. It's like turning it off and on again, a classic fix!

What if you click the 'AskChatGPT' button and nothing happens? This could be a sign-in issue. Make sure you're logged in to the right Microsoft account. Mixing up accounts is easy, especially if you have multiple accounts.

Some users might get stuck because the 'AskChatGPT' button is grayed out. This usually means there's a permission issue. Make sure your account has the rights to use all features in Word. It's like having a key—you need the right one to unlock everything.

Another common troublemaker is slow response times. This could be because of a slow internet connection. A good internet connection is like a fast-running stream—it makes everything flow smoothly.

If you're setting everything up right but ChatGPT is not responding as it should, it might be overwhelmed with requests. Sometimes, waiting a bit or trying during off-peak hours can make a difference.

Finally, if you're following the setup steps and it's still not working, reach out for help. There's a community and customer support ready to assist. Asking for help isn't a setback—it's a smart move to get you back on track.

Remember, every problem has a solution. Sometimes it takes a bit of patience and trying different things. But in the end, you'll have ChatGPT up and running in Word, ready to boost your productivity. Keep at it, and you'll get there!

29.3 Real-time Writing Assistance

Writing well matters. It's not just about getting the words down. It's also about how those words are strung together. This is where real-time writing assistance steps in. It's like having an invisible helper looking over your shoulder. This helper, ChatGPT, brings a toolbox filled with grammar checks, a thesaurus for the right word, and a translator for the world.

Grammar and Style Checks Using ChatGPT

Imagine writing without worry. No more fear of misplacing a comma. No anxiety over sentence structure. ChatGPT scans your text. It finds the little slips that could trip up your reader. It points out when a sentence is too long. It nudges you when the passive voice hides your meaning.

And style? That's about your voice. It's how you stand out. ChatGPT helps there too. It suggests techniques to make your writing clearer. More engaging. It protects the flow of your ideas. So, your voice comes through. Loud and clear.

Step 1: Start with Your Draft Write your piece. Don't worry about mistakes. Just get your ideas down.

Step 2: Activate ChatGPT Once your draft is ready, turn on ChatGPT. It's ready when you are.

Step 3: Scan for Errors ChatGPT will scan your text. It looks for grammar mistakes. It catches them fast.

Step 4: Review Suggestions ChatGPT shows suggestions. It gives you reasons too. This helps you learn.

Step 5: Apply Changes If you agree with a suggestion, apply it. It's just one click. Easy.

Step 6: Check for Style ChatGPT isn't just grammar. It's about style. It suggests changes to make your writing stronger.

Step 7: Finalize Your Document Review everything once more. If you're happy, you're done. Your document is now clear and correct.

Contextual Thesaurus and Vocabulary Suggestions

Next, let's talk words. The right word can be like the right key. It opens meanings. It unlocks emotions. ChatGPT works like a smart thesaurus. It doesn't just give synonyms. It considers the whole sentence. The context. It offers words that fit just right.

This is more than just swapping words. It's about enriching your writing. Making it vivid. With ChatGPT, your writing gains depth. It feels more alive. And you? You become a more powerful writer.

Step 1: Highlight the Word Find a word you want to change. Highlight it with your cursor.

Step 2: Ask ChatGPT With the word highlighted, ask ChatGPT for suggestions. It's like asking a friend.

Step 3: Review Options ChatGPT will offer synonyms. But not just any words. It picks ones that fit your sentence.

Step 4: Consider Context Look at your sentence. What are you trying to say? Choose a word that matches your meaning.

Step 5: Try It Out Pick a synonym. See how it fits. Read it out loud. Does it sound better?

Step 6: Decide If you like the new word, keep it. If not, try another. Or ask ChatGPT again.

Language Translation and Localization Assistance

Now, let's look beyond. Your words need to travel. They need to reach people in other countries. ChatGPT is your passport. It translates your writing into other languages. But it does more. It localizes it. This means it adapts your words. It makes them feel at home, anywhere.

This is crucial. Because a straight translation can be clunky. Even confusing. Localization looks at culture. It shapes your message. So, it fits. So, it's understood. With ChatGPT, your writing crosses borders. It becomes truly global.

Step 1: Choose Your Language First, tell ChatGPT which language you need. There are many to choose from.

Step 2: Translate the Text Ask ChatGPT to translate. It does it quickly. Your text now speaks another language.

Step 3: Look for Local Flavor. Translations can be stiff. Ask ChatGPT for localization. This adds local color.

Step 4: Review for Cultural Fit Check the translation. Does it respect the culture? Is it appropriate?

Step 5: Adjust if Necessary Sometimes, you'll want to tweak words. Make sure they're just right.

Step 6: Get Feedback if Possible If you can, find a native speaker. Ask them to review. They can catch things you might miss.

Step 7: Finalize Your Translation Once you're happy, and your text is clear, you're done. Your message is now global.

29.4 Workflow Automation

In the modern office, being smart with your time is crucial. Workflow automation is all about making the usual tasks quicker and more efficient.

Using ChatGPT to Automate Repetitive Tasks (e.g., Template Generation)

Step 1: Identify Repetitive Tasks Look at what you do every day. Find tasks you repeat often.

Step 2: Create a Template Make a standard version of a document you use a lot. This is your template.

Step 3: Open ChatGPT in Word Start ChatGPT in your Microsoft Word. It's ready to help.

Step 4: Instruct ChatGPT Tell ChatGPT to fill in your template with the needed info. Be clear about what goes where.

Step 5: Review the Completed Template ChatGPT will do the task and give you the filled template. Check it over.

Step 6: Save the New Document Save this new version for your use. Name it so you can find it easily later.

Step 7: Repeat as Needed Now, whenever you need a new document, ask ChatGPT to do it again.

Creating Custom Macros with ChatGPT for Complex Formatting Tasks

Step 1: Define the Formatting Task Think about the complex formatting you do. Decide exactly what you need.

Step 2: Access the Macros Feature In Word, go to the View tab, then click on Macros.

Step 3: Record a New Macro Choose to record a new macro. This is where ChatGPT will help.

Step 4: Perform the Formatting Do the formatting task as you usually would. ChatGPT will learn this.

Step 5: Stop Recording Once done, stop the recording. Your macro is now set.

Step 6: Edit the Macro with ChatGPT If needed, ask ChatGPT to edit the macro. It can make it more efficient.

Step 7: Use the Macro Now use this macro for your task. With one click, the job is done.

Scheduling and Reminder Integrations within Word Documents

Step 1: Write Down Your Schedule In your document, list your deadlines and important dates.

Step 2: Open ChatGPT Start ChatGPT and tell it about your schedule.

Step 3: Ask for Reminders Ask ChatGPT to remind you about these dates.

Step 4: Integrate with Calendar Link ChatGPT to your calendar. It will add these reminders for you.

Step 5: Set the Alert Times Choose when you want to be reminded. A day before? An hour before?

Step 6: Review Your Calendar Look at your calendar to see the reminders. Make sure they are right.

Step 7: Get Notified Now, when it's time, ChatGPT will remind you. You won't forget important tasks.

Summary of ChatGPT's Impact on Word Processing

ChatGPT has made a substantial mark on word processing. It is a robust tool that goes beyond simple text creation, extending its capabilities to editing, refining, and even translating content.

- **Grammar and Style Improvement**: The integration of ChatGPT in word processors has resulted in a noticeable decrease in grammatical errors and style inconsistencies.

- **Efficiency in Writing**: Writers can now produce content more quickly with ChatGPT's suggestions, which is especially beneficial for those facing tight deadlines.
- **Language Support**: Non-native speakers have found a valuable assistant in ChatGPT. It provides translations and localization, making writing in a second language easier.
- **Learning and Adaptation**: As an AI, ChatGPT learns from user interactions, constantly improving its suggestions and advice to better suit individual writing styles.

Future Potentials and Upcoming Features

The future of ChatGPT within word processing looks bright, with ongoing developments aimed at making writing more intuitive and efficient.

- **Predictive Writing**: ChatGPT can offer predictive writing features, suggesting entire paragraphs based on context.
- **Voice Command Integration**: Voice-to-text capabilities will likely become more advanced, allowing hands-free writing and editing.
- **Collaborative Features**: Real-time collaboration may become even smoother, with AI mediating discussions and suggesting edits among multiple users.
- **Document Accessibility**: ChatGPT is set to enhance document accessibility further, providing real-time assistance to individuals with disabilities.

30 CONCLUSION

Microsoft Word is more than just a word processor. It's a tool that can transform your work, making you more efficient and effective. For most people, mastering Word is about more than just impressing your bosses. It's about feeling confident in your skills and being the go-to person in your department. Microsoft Word has evolved over the years. With Microsoft 365, it's become even more powerful. The cloud integration means you can work from anywhere, anytime. And with the subscription model, you always have the latest features at your fingertips. But, like any tool, it's only as good as the person using it. Knowing how to install and set up Word is just the beginning. You need to understand its features and how to use them effectively. From creating and managing documents to advanced formatting, Word offers a range of options to help you work smarter. View options in Word, like light mode and dark mode, can make a big difference in how you work. They can reduce eye strain and make it easier to focus on your document. And the dashboard gives you quick access to all the tools you need. Formatting is crucial in Word. It's not just about making your document look good. It's about making it readable and accessible. Styles, numerations, and bulletins can help you structure your document, making it easier for your readers to follow. Find and Replace is a powerful tool in Word. It can save you hours of manual editing. And headers and footers can give your document a professional look, while also making it easier to navigate. Images and tables can bring your document to life. But they can also be tricky to format. Word offers tools to help you insert, edit, and format images and tables. And with the right techniques, you can make sure they enhance your document, rather than distract from it. Graphs and charts can help you present data in a clear and compelling way. And with Word's tools, you don't need to be a design expert to create professional-looking graphs and charts.

But even the most experienced Word users can run into problems. Temporary files can cause issues, and autosave settings can save over your work. Knowing how to troubleshoot these issues can save you time and frustration. Printing and exporting your document is the final step. But it's also one of the most important. Whether you're printing a report for a meeting or exporting a document to share online, you need to make sure it looks its best. Collaboration is a key feature of Word in Microsoft 365. With tools like Track Changes, you can work with colleagues in real time, no matter where they are. And with accessibility features, you can make sure your document is accessible to everyone. Security is crucial, especially when you're working with sensitive information. Word offers tools to help you protect your document, from password protection to permission management.

Macros can help you automate repetitive tasks, making you even more efficient. And with VBA, you can customize Word to fit your needs. Integration with other Microsoft Office applications can help you work even smarter. Whether you're pulling data from Excel or presenting with PowerPoint, Word can help you get the job done. And if you ever run into problems, Microsoft Support is there to help. With phone, chat, and email support, you can get the answers you need, when you need them.

Kevin Pitch

31 BONUS

Scanning the following QR code will take you to a web page where you can access several fantastic bonuses (video courses, templates, and a mobile app) after leaving your email contact. Your participation and feedback are greatly appreciated!
LINK: https://BookHip.com/TPWKHLD

Made in the USA
Monee, IL
21 November 2023

47074853R00092